the Skagway Connection

a spiritual journey

Lisa Brandom

MOON▲LAKE
PUBLISHING COMPANY
SILOAM SPRINGS, ARKANSAS

MOON▲LAKE
PUBLISHING COMPANY
14213 Lake Forrest Heights
Siloam Springs, AR 72761

The Skagway Connection: A Spiritual Journey. Copyright © 2005 by Lisa Brandom. All rights reserved. No part of this book may be reproduced in any form or by any electronic or mechanical means, including information storage and retrieval systems, without permission in writing from the publisher, except by a reviewer, who may quote brief passages in a review. Any members of educational institutions wishing to photocopy part or all of the work for classroom use, or publishers who would like to obtain permission to include the work in an anthology, should send their inquiries to Moon Lake Publishing Co., 14213 Lake Forrest Heights, Siloam Springs, AR 72761.

Printed in the United States of America

Design by Joel Armstrong, Photography by Garlan and Lisa Brandom

Library of Congress Cataloging-in-Publication Data
Brandom, Lisa
     The Skagway Connection: A Spiritual Journey / Lisa Brandom
        p. cm.
     ISBN 0-9755950-1-6

1. Brandom, Lisa—Childhood and youth
2. Authors, American—20th century—Biography
3. Christian Biography—United States

PS3552.R36S5 2005
818.5409 B734   2005107685

10 9 8 7 6 5 4 3 2
First Edition

to Garlan

for the way

to Mam, Mama, and Judy

for the truth

to Kimberly, Chris, Caitlyn, and Charlie

for the life

to Him

for the Way, the Truth, and the Life

"Wherefore, my beloved, as you have always obeyed, not as in my presence only, but now much more in my absence, work out your own salvation with fear and trembling."
Philippians 2:12
(New King James Version)

Part One:

The Odyssey

Chapter One
Oxymoron

My name is Lisa; this is my story; this is my song. While Ishmael could go on the great sea voyage with Captain Ahab in an attempt to capture the elusive white whale, at age fifty-four I know I'll have to discover another path. Instead of Melville's South Seas, I'll be going north instead, to Alaska, to search for the aurora borealis, to discover the nature of good and evil, of light and darkness, of summer and winter.

Ever since I was a child, I've been intrigued, and haunted, by the Skagway, Alaska, connection. I always spent summers in the early 1950s with Mam and Pop, my grandmother and her husband, Slick. I always considered him my real grandpa anyway since he had always been there. Besides, I had never known my paternal grandparents since they both died before I was born. Pop worked up and down the railroad as a section foreman for the Illinois Central Railroad in Tutwiler, Mississippi, located in the center of the Mississippi Delta.

They lived in what is commonly called a section house, provided by the railroad. Since the town had a population of just a thousand or so, the event of the day was for my older sister, Judy, and me to ride our bike to the post office, pick up the mail at Box 351, and go over to the drugstore for a cherry Coke. I said "our bike" because we had just one—a dilapidated blue, one-speed contraption that I'm sure my mother had bought secondhand for us. I can still hear in my mind the squeak of the wheels as Judy mounted the bike, and I plopped quickly on the handle-bars. It was always the same daily routine for this eight year old and a twelve year old. Since the post office was about a mile away, Judy would pedal to the Moore's house and stop precisely at their mailbox. As I rode on the handlebars, I hard-ly felt any breath of a breeze in the sultry, humid Mississippi heat. She'd then ride on the fraying seat of the bike with her long, skinny pre-adolescent legs splayed to the side while I stood up to pedal. At the Bruister's house, she'd take the final lap into town. I always thought I was the most put-upon and had the harder of the tasks since I was the little one.

"I can't go any fatha," I'd whine about halfway to the Bruister house.

"You'll just have to," Judy would unsympathetically respond as she yawned.

The cherry Coke, however, always provided a panacea, although a brief one, for the trip back to the section house. The soda guy, Gerald, was a middle-aged fellow who, like Pop, had always been around. Like the "Cheers" bar, and cer-tainly because it was a small town, he always knew our names and what we'd order (as well as all the others who'd be com-ing in during the day). He'd slide the frosty mugs over at us and growl, "That'll be a nickel." We learned later that he had this job only because he was a brother to the drugstore owner's wife, Mrs. Ragland. He drank a bit we heard from Mam, who would just shake her head and say, "Poor old Gerald. He's as shell-shocked from the war as anybody I've ever seen." Judy and I had no idea what that meant at the time. We imagined beach shells and couldn't imagine how they could be shocking to any-one. Nevertheless, Gerald prepared the endless requests from all the Tutwiler kids for cherry Cokes in the summer and for all the moviegoers before the nightly shows at the Tutrovansum. Admittedly, the show had a rather odd name but one that seemed perfectly understandable once Pop explained it to me.

"It's for all the names of the towns around us—Tutwiler, Rome, Vance, and Sumner. Somebody just put them all togeth-er in one big abbreviation," he drawled.

After the cherry Coke, the trip back on the bike seemed uneventful, and we were always hot, and certainly exhausted, when we burst into the back door. I don't remember ever using the front door (which faced the railroad tracks as if in obeisance to the god who provided Pop his and Mam's living).

"Mam," we'd holler as we came in the back door of the section house, "can we have a Coke?"

Early on, Judy and I had understood, I guess by osmosis, that Mam would never tell us no to anything. "Sure, ya'll go ahead and get some out of the freezer. Pop put some up there before he left this morning," Mam would respond to our question.

We knew there was some reason maybe she was so easy-going, but we never bothered at that time to initiate any prob-ing questions (obviously this was much before my adult interest in psychology that developed as I began to seek answers to life's big questions). Our own mother was a single mama who worked a double shift as a waitress in Greenville, some sixty miles or so away, and was just the opposite of Mam. I can still see Mama on a June afternoon between her split shift lying on the bed without her halter top on, a cold washrag on her chest, cooling off since we didn't have air conditioning back then. "One of ya'll get me some tea, would you? My jar's in the icebox," she'd command. Judy and I thought of different ways we could come into the house without going by her bedroom, but most of the time she could hear the door squeak anyway or the screen door slam. We knew exactly what the story was, though, behind her seeming oblivion to us, but we didn't like to think about those things while we were at Mam and Pop's. We rarely ever got Cokes at our apartment. There was a Chinese market down the alley and across the street, but when Mama sent us over there, we always had to come back with just the precise list of necessities she had ordered; otherwise, we'd have tons of explaining to do.

In our opinion, the next best drink ever to the cherry Coke we'd just consumed at the drugstore was its country cousin, the small, eight-ounce bottle of regular Coke (much before the new Coke came on the market years later only to be rejected by the majority of the buying public). Whenever we popped the lids off on the Coke opener on the back porch, we'd immediately look inside for the ice to form from having been in the freezer a couple of hours. By the time we'd finished those, Mam was calling us in to dinner, not lunch; only Yankees called the noon meal that. Pop had gotten in from his morning's work on the railroad, and the four of us sat down to the meal Mam had been literally sweating over all morning. It was not unusual for us to go into the kitchen while she was cooking to see her wiping the sweat with a dish towel as it was pouring down her face like the condensation on the Coke bottles we'd be drinking from. When Mama was in Tutwiler and helped Mam cook, she'd get so hot that whenever we'd sit down to eat, she'd announce, "I'm so hot I'm about to die. I can't eat right now. I've got to go lay down." We assumed that once again she'd take off her top and put a cold washrag on her chest to rest.

Mam always had on one of her favorite radio shows (and later TV shows, which she'd turn up several decibels louder than necessary in order to be able to hear it from the living room), like "The Guiding Light" or "As the World Turns," while she was cooking. She talked to the characters as if she knew them intimately. Often she was unaware that we were even in the room.

"You low-down Lisa, you!" I'd hear as I'd walk in the kitchen. I was a bit confused at first until I realized she was referring to Lisa Hughes, one of the long-time characters who was always hateful, it seemed, to her husband Bob, and couldn't get along with anybody at all.

Mam always cooked dinner with all the burners on the stove set on high. The oven would be set on 550 degrees to cook the cornbread, and then at the last minute Mam would call the broiler into action for the final browning of the top. Most of the time the cornbread would be a very dark brown with slivers of black encrusted everywhere. Since it was summer, we always had lots of fresh vegetables—tomatoes (which I didn't care for since once when I was quite small I had eaten airplane glue by mistake and read on the label that explosions could take place if placed near a fire. Since it was winter then, and we had space heaters, I just knew I was going to blow up. Judy said if I ate tomatoes I would throw up, and that would take care of the problem. Neither thing happened, fortunately, but I never liked tomatoes after that), fried okra, butter beans (not limas; only Yankees called them that), string beans (not green beans, again for the same reason as above), fried squash, and tons of other stuff. The meal was left on the stove after Pop went back to work on the railroad, and we ate the leftovers for supper that evening about four o'clock when Pop would quit work for the day.

After lunch, since the polio scare was a reality in the early 1950s, and just before Salk and Sabin made their eventful discoveries about vaccines, we had to lie down for two hours for a nap or reading. Somehow a nap was to help prevent the contraction of polio, although I'm not exactly sure what the connection was supposed to be. Now I think it was just maybe to give Mam a break from us (as was the daily post office run and the dip into her pocketbook for a nickel each for our cherry

Cokes). I was a typical Southern girl (now a past-middle-aged woman) who loved her naps from the very beginning, whereas Judy typically preferred to read. She read very quickly, and I was always in awe of her speed-reading but also a bit skeptical, and I insisted on asking her questions about her book to make her prove she'd really read it.

I'd take up the book and turn it randomly to page 141. "Who was the boy Susan was talking to about her ponytail?"

"She was telling Joe that it'd be a shame for her to cut her hair after it had taken four years to grow it past her waist and even if it did take half a day to dry she couldn't think of ever being without her ponytail. After all, that's what everybody who knew her said was her best asset—there now, Miss Smarty, are you satisfied?"

I was—but still dumbfounded at her phenomenal skill. I wasn't exactly envious though, even if I usually plodded very slowly through the biographies that I loved. I would enjoy and savor all the words of an especially good one like Madame Curie and would feel "chill bumps," as we say in the South, when she made her discovery of radium near the end of the book. My favorite biographies extended beyond the great ones like Abraham Lincoln (whom I admired greatly and told all my friends he was the best President ever because he freed the slaves, and I'd then be looked at rather sadly because everyone in the South in the 1950s was still fighting the Civil War and thought Abraham Lincoln was the sole cause of our big defeat). I liked the sports heroes best, especially if they had conquered over-powering obstacles to reach their success. Lou Gehrig was a man to be admired, more in my opinion, for his courageous fight against a horrendous disease that would take his life, far before it seemed necessary, to me. I thrilled to his words that day when he retired and stood in Yankee Stadium saying, "Today I am the luckiest man on the face of the earth." I liked Glenn Cunningham's story, overcoming all those crippling cir-cumstances related to his burned legs, to become one of the world's fastest runners at that time. After completing each one, it then became my latest favorite.

Judy and I always took a huge stack of books, which we had checked out from the Greenville Public Library, to Mam and Pop's house. The idea of actually buying books would have been totally out of the question at this point in our lives. Our apartment with Mama was about a mile or so from our library, which was near the levee in Greenville. The library was housed in an old building on a quiet, oak tree-lined street. The entry steps were framed by two lion sculptures, which seemed to threaten rather than welcome potential library patrons. The librarians at this particular library were a bit like the lions: "Children, don't ever shelf the books yourselves!" they would scream in their loudest whispering voices. "Ya'll will get everything out of order," they'd tell us as they pounced around their lairs, menacing the other children as well. Judy and I, therefore, checked out our books as quickly as possible and left. We could check out as many as we wanted for two full weeks. Sometimes we could hardly carry them back home, but again, because Judy was a faster reader, she usually got far more than I. I, along with the great Richard Wright as reported in his autobiographical essay, "The Library Card," developed a voracious appetite for words and stories and even scents of the library. Even today the smell of old books makes my mind return to my childhood. I see myself, instead of at an Alcoholic Anonymous meeting, confessing to a group of fellow bibliomaniacs, "My name is Lisa, and I'm a full-fledged book lover. I neglect my family…."

When the obligatory, but ultimately enjoyable, nap time was over for Judy and me, the best time of the day began. I usually did one of three favorite activities—go outside and sit in the grass (sometimes there'd still be clover and I could make necklaces from the accompanying flowers, which I'd slit at the bottom of the stem and string together foot after foot, or search for the four-leaf varieties since I knew our family needed some luck) or just lie on my back gazing at the cumulus clouds for a while, first imagining the ever-changing shapes were various plants, animals, and even God Himself and then imagining myself actually being lifted from earth and floating up to join the clouds in play like the little child in Blake's *Introduction to The Songs of Innocence.* One of my other favorite activities was sure to follow since by that time I was usually a bit bored.

I'd then call for Judy to come out and join me for a tea

party—only it wasn't exactly that; it was an imitation of the Lord's Supper (not Communion; only high churches called it that and certainly not dyed-in-the-wool Southern Baptists like us). Since Judy was approaching age thirteen in a few more months, I'm sure she just indulged me in my childhood games. We'd go into Mam's refrigerator, take out the bottle of Welch's grape juice she always had on hand, and get some saltine crackers from the cupboard. Our favorite glasses were the little shot glasses that we found up front in the cupboard. We'd then sit at a table in the backyard of the section house (which Mam and Pop would use for summer picnic times) and pretend we were drinking the blood of Christ and eating the body of Christ.

Next I'd go back into the house and holler again at my grandmother (Judy would go back to reading her books), "Mam, can I go through your drawers?"

"Sure you go right ahead. Mam don't care if you just search and search to your heart's content. Have yourself a heap of fun," she'd say.

Since I stayed every summer with Mam and Pop, I knew where all the fun stuff was at her house. I already knew the contents of every nook and cranny, but it was always fun to explore again. My third activity centered on what Mam called the "boo-fay" (it was only after I became an adult that I realized she meant "buffet") and an old trunk on the back porch, which Pop had carried home with him from the wars, both World Wars, I and II. Both contained the most wonderful secrets from a past life that didn't seem at all to fit the reality of their present lives. The sides of the boo-fay held letters that Pop had evidently typed and sent to Mam during the war (II since they didn't know each other in I). I was always impressed that a man could type at that time, though not well, and that must have been part of the fascination too. The one that I kept going back to again and again was dated just three days after I was born in 1944—November 8. It was sent from a place called Skagway, Alaska. It began, "My Darling Wife, Have Been Wondering If You Made The trip O.K.. NO News from You since you began your trip, i was at lea st expecting a wire up on your arrival in st, paul.Darling i Do hope you made every thing all right, you dont know how lomesome it is with out you here. . . ." Could this be MY Pop I wondered as I compared the romantic words to the old, balding man with a potbelly that I now knew as Pop. I was also especially intrigued by the contents of the trunk. Once the lid was open (I was as excited as Pandora must have been), I found the uniforms and the hats and the medals from his time in the service, but there was also the oddest-looking money I had ever seen—Japanese money. "Not any good any more," Pop would say.

The top of the trunk had a lid with small items in it, and there was a scrapbook with tons of pictures and important-looking old papers already yellowing with age, a mere eight years after the war. I couldn't believe the photograph of Mam with her black hair, rather than the white I had always known her to have. She and Pop would be sitting at what appeared to be a club with tons of other people, and they seemed to be DRINKING. I knew Mam and Pop had those shot glasses in their house (with "Skagway, Alaska" printed on them), but I had never actually seen them drink. "Could it be possible?" I wondered. In the scrapbook, I found a menu from the Victoria • Vancouver • Skagway Service, which named the most exotic items I had ever heard of—steamed chicken halibut (I wondered how that could be), potato croquettes (up until this time I had known only of salmon croquettes), celery en branche (certainly that couldn't be just plain old celery), pork pie (I had read about that but only in Dickens' novels like when Pip was rummaging through his sister's cupboards to feed the convict Magwitch out in the bog), wine jelly (surely not; it must have been a typo), and my favorite of all—boiled ox tongue served with caper sauce, apple fritters, and lemon sauce. I found newspaper clippings about the war and the work on the railroad in Alaska as well as countless postcards of Skagway, a quaint little town at the foot of high, snow-capped mountains; Whitehorse, an icy-looking place in Canada; and places called Lake Bennett, White Pass, and Yukon.

The hidden items of the boo-fay and the trunk weren't the only reminders I had that there existed a place far beyond the humid and sweaty confines of the Mississippi Delta. It was my job (I'm sure this was Mama's idea and not Mam's) to dust every day while we were at our grandparents' house.

Judy got the better job in my opinion and got to vacuum. Back then housekeeping seemed to be more revered than it apparently is now, and dusting was a chore that had to be done every day of the week (maybe with the exception of Sunday when the four of us went to First Baptist Church together in Tutwiler). The coffee table wasn't a bad job as there was perhaps just one or two items placed on it. One was an ashtray made out of whalebone, which also sported the words "Skagway, Alaska" on the outside. It didn't matter how careless I was with the dust rag, knocking the ashtray over numerous times; it seemed indestructible. My unfavorite item to dust was what Mam called Pop's "whatnot" shelf. It contained a lot of little Woolworth's items that Judy and I had bought Mam and Pop for Christmas and special occasions, but there were also more evidences of that elusive place called Skagway.

"Mam, what was it like to live in Skagway?" I'd inquire.

"Oh, it was a heap of fun up there...." and then she'd go on to describe some of her numerous memories of her trip in the midst of the war to be with her husband for a few months back in 1944. He had been the commanding officer of Company A of the 770th Railway Battalion. Mam's eyes would then begin to twinkle like Santa's, and she would get a strange, far away look in her eyes. I thought at times they would even begin to mist a little, and her smile would begin to resemble that of Mona Lisa. I figured there was something she wasn't telling me, but I couldn't figure out what. As for me, I couldn't believe there was a part of the U.S. (though not officially until a few years later in 1959) where the weather could be so extremely cold (maybe even thirty degrees below zero in the dead of winter) compared to the Mississippi Delta, especially in the summertime. I couldn't fathom the stories of the continual daylight and the bright lights called the aurora borealis.

"Mam, how can you go to sleep if it's light outside all the time?" I'd inquire.

I certainly couldn't imagine my grandmother riding in a Jeep named Lillian at all, although I had seen the picture of her smiling in the sporty little vehicle numerous times. She called it her buggy and said the wind nearly blew her out at times. I giggled incessantly when she told the story of losing her false teeth as she rounded a corner in Skagway one day a bit too fast. The contrasts were almost too overwhelming for me. I knew I'd have to explore this intriguing place for myself one day and learn of its secrets. I'd go on an Odyssey I told myself—not necessarily one to return home to my spouse, Penelope, or my child, Telemachus,—but to recover my lost innocence—if indeed such a quality as innocence truly exists.

Chapter Two
Odysseys

It seems to me that Odysseus' journey was much more than a physical one. He's the one who developed the masterful plot to end the Trojan War with his idea of the gigantic Greek horse. Because of this (and other reasons), Dante would later show Odysseus in Hades being miserably tortured with the other evil counselors. Perhaps if he had not been such a big braggart about his love conquests with Calypso and his overwhelming mental victory over the giant Cyclops, Polyphemus, the gods might have had more mercy on him. He definitely fought a number of spiritual battles.

I'm not sure exactly when my spiritual battles began, but I do know that I became aware of little sins on my third birthday. Since I am a "born and bred" Southern Baptist, as they say in the South, I didn't have to be taught to be naughty; it certainly seemed to be an innate characteristic. Mama and Daddy were living in Greenville in a little apartment with a ditch running behind it. My "boyfriend" Robert, whom I loved as dearly as one could love at the age of three, and I were excited about the chocolate cake my mother was icing for me. We both stood on our tiptoes peeping over the high kitchen table where Mama had just placed the cake in front of our eyes. Law officers today would agree that our soon-to-be crime would fall into the category of an attractive nuisance—like leaving a purse in the front seat of a car, clearly visible to a would-be criminal. As Flip Wilson would say, (and earlier supported by Adam and Eve's comment in the Garden), "The devil made us do it."

Mama left the room to do her daily chores, and Robert and I systematically initiated the cake attack, using our pinkies to scoop up one delectable bite after another until we had simply robbed all the icing from the cake. It sat there naked as one without the decency of proper clothing. We must have been convicted about the same time of our crime, or maybe because we were just full of the gooey, sweet icing, but we stopped and stared at each other for the briefest of moments and went tearing out the back door to hide in the ditch behind the house—away, we hoped, from Mama's inevitable wrath. I'm not sure how long we stayed, but eventually I could hear Mama's voice. "Martha Elise, come here this instant," she yelled in that godlike voice all our mothers share and the one we have all dreaded in our childhood.

As we sneaked quietly back into the house, Mother began the interrogation. "What happened to this cake? Did ya'll do this?"

"No'am," I whimpered, in the tiniest of all possible voices, forgetting that I had the sticky evidence of my crime all over me—mouth, hands, clothes, and even hair. Thankfully, Daddy came in from work shortly after that with his easygoing, loping gait and boyish smile (but only if he were sober). He brushed the crime aside, declared it a misdemeanor, and

soon he and Mama were giggling at two three year olds trying to get a head start on the party.

A mere six weeks or so later, the scene had deteriorated.
Both my parents had moved from giggles to tears, from temporary peace to an undeclared war for us as a family. Tillie
Olsen's "I Stand Here Ironing" always reminds me now of
Mama that Christmas. She, like the protagonist in that story,
also stood in her apartment ironing. It was in our tiny backroom
apartment at 633 Central that she was crying, at first quietly and
then evidently quite loudly as she ironed Judy's and my school
dresses. Daddy had been off on a job, Christmas was a couple of
days away, and as usual, Mama didn't know if or when he'd be
back. Since the rooms were wafer-thin in the house, the landlady likely heard Mama's periodic sobs and heaves for breath
and came over to inquire what the problem was.

"Mike's gone, and I don't have anything for my kids—
not even any food," she managed to say, hunching over, with
her head so far down to the ironing board she might have lost
her balance.

I'm sure the landlady had already given Mama some lee-
way in her rent payments since this was our typical situation,
rather than an atypical one. Mama's letters at that time indicated that she was always walking five or six miles away to rent
an apartment while Daddy kept Judy and me in a temporary
room he was renting, and the three of us took a nap. She often
had to talk the latest landlady into accepting a few days rent

instead of a week's and even loaning us her own dishes and linens until she could get her boxes shipped by bus to the new place. I'm sure this landlady was no exception to the type Mama had dealt with in the past. I often think these women must have been like Mama in many ways—living without men in their lives, and were perhaps even widows—trying to make it themselves by dividing their houses into apartments in the late 1940s. They could also understand what need for a woman means (and how it differs from a man's) and the hopelessness of not being able to provide for your kids.

As a three year old, I , of course, was unaware of the drama being played out in our apartment that Christmas. I just knew Christmas was coming, and the desire of my three-year-old spirit was to have a dollhouse with two stories and little toy furniture and people that I could move from room to room. Actually, I don't think I had even told Santa Claus this wish. I know I hadn't told Mama.

The landlady patted Mama and hugged her, telling her everything was going to work out okay.

Not more than two hours after the landlady left, we heard loud knocking at the side door, "Boom, boom, boom." We didn't know if it was the police bringing Daddy in again drunk or someone perhaps to evict us for all of our debts, like in Tiny Tim's family. Evidently, however, the landlady had called Second Baptist Church in Greenville, knowing that they had several Christmas ministry programs. Two men stumbled in carrying several sacks of groceries for us and a large hen for our Christmas dinner.

The miraculous surprise, though, was they brought exactly the dollhouse for me that I had been dreaming of. I sat there playing with it for hours after they had gone, and in my unconscious mind, I was sure I was like the family I'd later read about at my school across the street when I was in first grade—there was Mother, Father, Dick, Jane, and even a dog named Spot.

When I was five, I learned more about the nature of sin and God's grace. Instead of just sneaking icing from a cake and lying about it, I now became aware of an inward sin, which nobody can see. By this time Mama and Daddy were separated, and Mama was working as a waitress. At first she hired a young Negro girl, just barely a teenager herself, to take care of us while she was gone. We loved Era Mae. She played with us and laughed with us all the time, but she could cook us only one supper—grits. Every day for weeks we ate grits. Mama would come in at midnight, wake up Era Mae, and send her home in a cab.

Since Judy was nine now, Mama decided we were old enough to stay by ourselves if she checked on us by phone several times during the evening, and we knew we could call her at any time as well—even during the busiest of rush times. We usually did.

"Mama, Lisa won't do the dishes," Judy would complain to her over the phone.

"Let me speak to her then."

I'd stroll to the phone at my leisure. "I did them last night," I'd whine.

"You did not. You liar you," Judy would retort.

The conversation would go on until Mama usually said she had to go and would arbitrarily choose one of us to do the dreaded dishwashing chore for the evening.

On one particular occasion, we were alone in the late afternoon on a summer's day (though it seems practically every day in Mississippi year round could fall into that category). Judy and her friends were sitting on the steps in front of the apartment—still at 633 Central. They were playing games of some sort like jacks, or perhaps even Monopoly. I, on the other hand, was more of a loner and a tough girl than anything else, in my opinion. I was tremendously proud of my new red tricycle, which was all my own, and was doing my own version of wheelies back and forth across the graveled driveway beside the house. It was not until many years later when I saw Leonardo DiCaprio as Jack that he gave me the line to express the feeling I had that day—with the self-made breeze combing gently through my hair and the elevation of pride in myself for all my minute conquests as I repeatedly raced across the drive—"I'm king of the world." In the middle of one of my wheelies, the tricycle flipped over as quickly as a fall leaf tumbling under the oak trees in the yard and threw me face first into the gravel in the drive. Unfortunately, a garbage truck, one with those gigantic double wheels on each side in the back, had also begun to back out of the drive at the same time. I distinctly remember seeing the wheels coming toward me and then making a merciless groaning sound as they attempted to career over my back.

By this time Judy and her friends had seen my plight and were screaming and gesticulating frantically at the truck driver, "Stop, Mister, stop! There's a kid down there!" He did and later said that he was unaware that I was even there under the wheels, but the other kids were creating such a commotion that he knew something was wrong. I came out of this experience unscathed—nursing just a few scratches. My new red tricycle, on the other hand, was crunched.

The immediate concern for Judy and me was to swear to secrecy. Mama simply couldn't know what happened that day; she would cry. It wasn't until we were adults that we told her, and—she cried. It was at this time that I could sense I had a destiny beyond what I could then see. While I didn't know anything whatsoever about theology, I had this definite notion that I had been spared somehow for a purpose even larger than myself.

One of my earliest memories relating to church was attending Second Baptist Church in Greenville with Mama and Judy. That we chose this church wasn't a surprise since we had seen true Christianity revealed that Christmas morning when I was three. I couldn't have been more than seven or eight when I went to Sunday School with other boys and girls my age. I remember once my teacher was sharing with us the parable about the rich man going away for a time and, in his absence, leaving his three servants with specific instructions. Evidently he gave each of his servants differing amounts of talents—one five, another two and another one.

"Now, boys and girls," my middle-aged, rather rotund teacher with horned-rimmed glasses said to us as we sat around those short, squatty tables, "the one servant who had five talents now had five additional ones; the servant who had two now had two more; but the servant who had been given just one didn't have another one. He told his master that he had gone out and buried his talent. Boys and girls, who do you think the master was the most proud of?"

No sounds were heard around the table for a brief second; then, I thrust my hand up into the air as quickly as I possibly could.

"Lisa?"

"The one who buried his because he hadn't lost it for the master."

I felt my response was perfectly reasonable in light of the fact that money was so hard to come by in my family. Why shouldn't he put it away and save it for a later day? How could I be expected to know anything about depositing money with bankers and interest accruing? How could my mother know anything about it when she earned just $3 a day at her job? She did get tips, thankfully, and she worked a split shift to serve both dinner and supper to earn more. Her record book in Greenville in 1952 reflects her tips from March 30 to April 5 at the Park Inn Grill and looks like this:

Sunday	$1.70
Monday	2.85
Tuesday	3.30
Wednesday . . .	3.00
Thursday	1.05
Friday	2.96
Saturday	4.15

$19.01

A mere two weeks later she had started another job at Huckabee's Steak House. Later she would work at Evon's Steak House and at Azar's after that. Mama changed jobs a lot, always hoping for a place where she could make better tips. I didn't always appreciate her work as a child; for one reason, when she took Judy and me to church, we had to sit on the back row. About a quarter to twelve, she would slip out, go to the bathroom and change into her waitress uniform, grab a cab, and be off to work for the noon shift. I did always think she looked pretty then with her crisp, white uniform on with her coal black, longish hair and her real red lipstick on. Judy and I would be left either to walk back to our apartment—about a mile or two away, or if we were especially blessed that day, to get invited over to the Truitt's house for dinner. The Truitts were members of Second Baptist also, and Judy and I were friends with their two girls, Hilda and Lillian. They also had a younger brother, Robert, but we didn't pay any attention to him. He was just a spoiled rotten pest in our opinion (as was every other boy we knew since it was obvious that their fathers doted on them to the exclusion of us girls).

Mrs. Truitt served fried chicken every Sunday with mashed potatoes and gravy, whereas our own mama's meals were different. She would usually bring home from the noon rush some cold mashed potatoes maybe, or some ham, cornbread, or whatever the restaurant had an abundance of. We liked it hot at Mrs. Truitt's.

Today, as I look at Mama's record book, a story is being told as clearly in numbers just as it might be in words and ideas that we label today as signifiers and signified, interspersed with tons of similes and metaphors. I notice that she always started her week off with Sunday; it was the first day of the week to her rather than the Sabbath. As an eight year old, I didn't realize that Mama didn't have a day off. Her tip book reveals, though, that she worked all seven days of the week. Mama and Daddy had been officially divorced in 1950, although they had been separated for some time before that. According to the final divorce decree on October 3, he was to pay $60 a month for our support. We never hoped for any money from him though, so we always felt we needed to celebrate when he sent us any at all.

Other people, like one of her waitress friends Pearl, who knew of our struggle to survive at that time, would often ask her why she didn't just have Daddy (Mike to her) thrown into jail and be done with it. She'd just reply, "Oh, Lord, that'd be like squeezing blood from a turnip. He doesn't have a dime either, and what good would that do us?" I now know that the truth was she loved him then, and to the end of her life, and that such an action would have been impossible. She blamed herself for the breakup of the marriage since he always told everyone she drove him to drink.

I did notice in the tip book that Mama seemed to be going through a crisis of some type since she didn't work for nine full days the latter part of August and the first part of September in 1952. No tips were recorded, and she simply wrote the word "off." Mam and Pop evidently gave us $20 to tide us through the dips in tips and salary. It might have been the start, or perhaps the continuation, of the emotional problems that would plague her all her life. She would check into the hospital rather frequently, and she would be in bed more and more, not just during the day with her washrag across her chest but all night too. Judy and I had no conception of what "normal" was though at that time; we just knew that she was our Mama and that was our normality; she was the only Mama we had besides Mam, of course, in the summer.

It was not uncommon in Mama's tip book to see her bills listed beside her tips to the right—phone, drug, Dr. Reid (our dentist whom we had a running account with it seemed and never had a zero balance, but who evidently was gracious enough to extend credit to a single mother), hospital insurance, burial insurance, life insurance, and rent. Daddy usually never forgot us though at Christmas. Mama recorded $40 in 1952 in the week of Dec. 14 to Dec. 20. The next week of Christmas she listed the money she had received (again likely a gift to the three of us from Mam and Pop—$5.00, $6.00 and $2.00—or perhaps it was from her boss at work or some grateful customers for her efficient service seven days a week).

If a stranger were looking at the tip book, he or she might not understand the reference periodically to the "jar." It was almost as if the "jar" was personified with a life of its own when she'd record, "jar owes me 20 cents" or "owe jar $4 from last week." The jar was an old jelly container that Mama kept on the top shelf in the kitchen. The week of Mar. 29 to April 4, she recorded that she "Put $2 in jar for revival," and the next week had 50 cents in the jar. It was typical for her to come home from her waitress job at midnight and spread her tips on the kitchen table, carefully putting nickels, dimes, quarters, and pennies into the jar—which represented our tithe and gifts to the church or other community-based organizations like the Community Chest. If there's one subject one hears a lot about in a Southern Baptist Church, it's tithing.

I never felt Mama wanted to do anything, though, but to give her tithe gladly because she literally believed that giving would mean the rest of the tips would go farther during the next week. Judy and I always felt like " big shots," as Daddy would say, when we put $1 each into the offering at church every Sunday when our friends would give a nickel or so. We also got to fill up our March of Dimes cards the quickest of anyone at Ella Darling Elementary School since that money came from the jar as well.

Even though I had become aware of outward sin at the tender age of three and then again at five (a bit before the age of accountability of twelve as defined by the Southern Baptist denomination), I didn't understand the concept of salvation, or feel the necessity of it until I was nine. The time was February of 1954. Brother Perry, our preacher (not pastor), had invited an evangelist for a two-week revival at the church. It was Sunday morning, and Mama had done her usual disappearing act for work about 11:45 just before the "invitation." The invitation, for those who don't understand what I mean, is a time in our Baptist churches when the Holy Spirit is likely to speak to us individually, telling us that Jesus Christ died for our sins and that we need to come forward publicly in church and proclaim our belief in Him before God and everyone.

I distinctly remember the evangelist pleading with the congregation to do just that—in our church we believe "once saved, always saved"—and don't have a lot of patience with other denominations who believe differently. The pastor was saying, "While I can't predict the future, no one can, some of you might be hearing this plea for the last time. You don't know what might happen this very day. You could be killed and might never have a chance to accept Jesus again. You would go straight to hell, folks, if that happened. I don't want to scare you, but if you feel the Holy Spirit speaking to you, you MUST NOT say no to Him. Choir, let's sing another verse!"

By this time I was feeling mightily convicted and didn't feel I could keep my feet from stepping out into the aisle and walking down and grasping Brother Perry's hand, telling him I had just accepted Jesus as my Lord and Savior. But...I always knew I had to ask Mama about big decisions. I figured that she had just about enough time to get to her job at Azar's, so I (sitting in our usual back pew) went out the rear of the church to the pay phone in the hall (not foyer) and called her.

"Mama, I'm still at church, and I've just got to go down and get saved today."

"Lisa, we need to talk some more about this before you do that. Just go on home, and we'll talk later this afternoon when I get off."

"O.K." I replied and walked back into the church auditorium (we don't usually say sanctuary in the South).

If one knows anything about Baptist churches, he or she knows that the invitation can go on for verse after verse, and usually the song being sung endlessly is either "Just As I Am" or "Softly and Tenderly." The congregation was still singing; the evangelist was still pleading. I didn't stop at the pew where Judy was seated; I just kept on walking and grasped Brother Perry's hand and told him, "I came to be saved!"

Now, some forty-five years later as I reflect on these memories and God's faithfulness through the best of times and even through the worst of times (as Charles Dickens would say), I wonder how I ever got from point A as a believer to point B (not an unbeliever, because I still believe in Southern Baptist theology of never losing one's salvation), but I'm definitely an occasional skeptic and doubter of traditional theology. As a child in Sunday School, I never thought I would identify quite so much with doubting Thomas, the apostle. I too now want some real-life, physical evidence, to feel the nail prints in His hand. That's why my own personal Odyssey is so necessary for me now. I feel I can also identify with the angst of modern heroes like Binx in *The Moviegoer* as well as with classical heroes like Odysseus.

At the beginning of Binx's search for the meaning of life, he attempts to clarify and explain his position: "The search is what anyone would undertake if he were not sunk in the everydayness of his own life.... To become aware of the possibility of the search is to be onto something. Not to be onto something is to be in despair.... What do you seek—God? you ask with a smile."

Even old Odysseus (Ulysses as he's known in Italy) tried to defend to Dante in Hades his position. He inspired his men with these words, "'Shipmates,' I said, ' who through a hundred thousand / perils have reached the West, do not deny / to the brief remaining watch our senses stand / experience of the world beyond the sun. / Greeks! You were not born to live like brutes,

/ but to press on toward manhood and recognition!'"

What will I find as I go to Skagway for my search or odyssey? What, or who, has led me to this place in my life? Where, like Odysseus, will I confront the giants in my life who now threaten to separate me from God, even though He's promised me in Romans never to let that happen?

Part Two

Limbo

Chapter Three
Grave Thoughts

"Mama, you know I've been mad at God for nearly a decade now," I whisper in my mind, as I stand by her graveside at Washington Memorial Gardens with my husband, Garlan. Our odyssey to Alaska had begun six weeks earlier on the morning of June 6 as we left our home in northwest Arkansas for our destination, and this visit to the cemetery seemed essential. Her birthday is two days away—on July 16. We have come to place a flowering gloxinia with deep pink blossoms on her grave in remembrance.

The graveside is located just across the road from a praying hands statue and underneath a large tree. Mama was always a believer in answered prayer even if it took years longer than expected for the answers to come. The site is on a bit of a hill, but since Seattle is mostly cloudy and gray the year round, I don't think I've ever seen the full view.

She chose this site with Nelson, her second husband, because of its peacefulness, no doubt, and the fact that it's located just to the east of the SeaTac International Airport. Airplanes were doubly important to her since Nelson worked for Boeing Aircraft Company from 1960 until his retirement in 1984, but they were also the means by which she could get home to the South to see her girls every year for a visit. She'd often say to us, "I prayed, 'Lord, I'm willing to go anywhere for You—even to the ends of the earth.' And wouldn't you know? He very nearly sent me to the end of the earth here in Seattle!"

I look down to admire the stone, made of pink granite. It is a double one with her side giving the date of her birth and the date of her death in February of 1993. The Scripture verse is taken from Psalms 46: 1: "God is our refuge and strength, a very present help in trouble." Nelson's side of the stone has just his date of birth—1921. He is now a resident at Judson Park, a nursing facility in Des Moines. The doctors have moved him there in the past year and one-half from the two other wings of the facility (which are designed for patients needing less care) to what I call "the final waiting area."

The final waiting area—that's where we'll all be in time, I think. As for me I'm not in a hurry to go to it, and beyond it, until I can settle a bit of the unfinished business here on earth with God. I know Mama can't answer my questions directly about my confusion and skepticism, but nevertheless I feel her presence as surely as Hamlet felt the ghost of his father—directing and giving advice.

I think my questions began in 1989, in the summer of my 44th year, when I discovered that our son, Chris, had started drinking and had been doing so since he was 15. I'm sure I overreacted.

"How could you break my heart like this?" I screamed at him as we sat by the pool in the backyard where we lived in Tontitown, Arkansas.

I guess I thought it was all about me instead of him. And it was—in my mind. Daddy had been a compulsive gambler when he and Mama married in 1937. She knew it, but he had promised to change, and she believed him. His vow to forgo the excitement of shooting craps, as he called it, lasted for just a week. Within the next few years, he had slept with a number of other women (even married a few of them) and had become addicted to alcohol.

When Garlan and I married, I was so determined that my children would have a perfect life. I even imagined in my mind that I was perfect. I wanted us to be like the storybook family that I had played with at age three (when the Second Baptist Church members brought the dollhouse in to me for Christmas). My ideal consisted of the plastic doll figures of Mama, Daddy, and two children in a beautiful house with many rooms. If I had been more self-aware then, I would have realized that, while beautiful, they weren't alive.

I had thought I would ensure success spiritually for my children by enrolling them early on in the Christian school connected to our church, First Baptist in Springdale. When both were five and one respectively, a James Robinson revival was held in Fayetteville at the Barnhill Arena (otherwise the home of the Arkansas Razorback basketball team). I remember that time was especially meaningful in my life because Kimberly went forward to accept Jesus as her Savior. She was so young, but she seemed to understand the basic concept that she was a sinner in need of God's grace.

Another memory I have is that Robinson stated to us that the only possession we can take with us to heaven is our children. I wrote that statement down and put it on my mirror in the bedroom for years, knowing that it was absolutely true.

Yet here was Chris before me now—admitting that he had been drinking with his friends for at least a couple of years. I knew the results of the research studies, which pointed out a heredity link between children, and even grandchildren, of alcoholics. I panicked. I knew drinking was an escape. But what was he trying to escape from? As I saw it, he had a perfect life.

"Why are you doing this?" I quizzed.

"Because it's fun. There's no other reason," he replied nonchalantly.

Over the next several years, the pattern again became much like that with Daddy and Mama. There would be tears on my part, accusations, threats, promises to do better with letting go and trusting more—but with no significant change.

I didn't blame Chris' choices entirely on heredity though. I think I was typical of a lot of working mothers in the 1970s and 1980s who felt we could do it all—career and homemaking—without a glitch. I began to realize I couldn't. I had taught for years at the same Christian school where Kimberly and Chris were students, teaching at a salary several thousand dollars below public school teachers. I had a doctorate, yet it was good to be with the children at all times and know exactly what they were doing, where they were going, and with whom. I needed control, and I liked it.

In 1987, I had started a new position as registrar at a private liberal arts college twenty miles away. It was a difficult adjustment to work year round and to be away when Chris was just entering high school. Just maybe if I had still been around at Shiloh (the high school), I told myself, I could have heard rumors from other students or overseen his behavior more. Who knows?

In the meantime, Kimberly, our daughter, who also had a perfect life in my opinion, seemed to be the perfect daughter. She was studious and bright, an English major like myself. Her dream was to go to California and perhaps do some acting or go to graduate school after she completed her degree at the University of Arkansas. I longed almost to join her because I guess I had inherited a restless spirit from Daddy and had been living in the same town so long. But at age forty-four, on a hot August morning, I let her go. I watched as she got into her 1984 Pontiac Sunbird with her friend, Lorie, and headed west toward Los Angeles. In 1991, she came home and confided that she was a lesbian. As with Chris, I found myself putting me, not her, into the center of the discussion. From what I've read and heard, I'm sure my reaction was even worse than Cher's when her daughter, Chastity, also shared the same news.

"What you're doing, Kimberly, is just rebelling. If you think about it, you dated Brian, the marijuana head; Tony, the agnostic; Osbed, the Armenian; and David, the Jew. It appears this is another one of your little phases!" I yelled as I had with Chris just two years earlier. "What will people think of me if they find out? Promise me that you won't tell anyone around here ever. I'd be so embarrassed," I cajoled.

The primary reason for my reaction wasn't that I didn't love her anymore. How could I believe she had changed any by the utterance of those four little words? It was that our church's teachings seemed clear on the issue. We had known for years THE list in I Corinthians 6, verse 9. The ones who wouldn't inherit the kingdom of God included homosexuals (as well as drunkards). Romans 1:26 spoke of women and vile passions, exchanging "the natural use for what is against nature." The Old Testament verses were too numerous to cite.

Even though I knew I loved both Kimberly and Chris unconditionally, I needed a while to get over my anger primarily at God. With Kimberly I had seen signs of her boyish behavior early on—she never liked to wear dresses, especially the frilly, lacy ones that her MeMa made for her. She was very athletic and sporty, and she always expressed her desire to be a boy. I had simply done my dead level best, as we say in the South, to make sure she had no idea what homosexuality was. We never spoke of it, and I was sure no one at Shiloh had either. I encouraged her to like boys, to flirt as I had stupidly as a young woman, never to know anything else was possible.

Yet here she was before me—wanting my love as she

always had and later feeling suicidal when she felt I was rejecting her.

I had prayed since she was a child that she would not be a lesbian—simply because life is so hard in a society that marginalizes gays. I had prayed for the spouses both she and Chris would marry. When she came out to me that night in 1991, I was mad at God. Why had He not answered my prayers?

I remember talking on the phone to Mama in Seattle, who sent me a book by Ruth Graham called *Prodigals and Those That Love Them.* It told of Ruth's own struggle with her son, Franklin, who seemed to be so far away from God in his younger years and of her unconditional love of him. I remember what Mama said to me about Kimberly, "That's not going to change how we feel about her."

It was at this time that another spiritual battle began in relationship to my faith, and the old, pat answers of my faith seemed to be failing me. I spent a lot of hours thinking, crying, praying for God to help me understand. As a teacher for the past twenty-five years, I reflected on all the children I had seen and taught who were far too young to know anything about sexuality, but had displayed overt characteristics of the opposite sex. As they became adults, I knew exactly which ones were gay and which ones were straight. It was as if I had "gaydar" as one of my lesbian students would later tell me. Concurrently, studies from science and psychology were exploring the causes of homosexuality and concluding more and more that one was born one way or another. Instead of some Freudian, Oedipal explanation as we had been given in the past, scientists were deleting their "abnormal" sections of the textbooks and rewriting them to indicate that some one to ten percent of the population was gay; it was an orientation, not a perversion.

My primary question for God then, and even now, is, "God, if you created my child this way, how could you condemn what You Yourself have made?" The issue is such a controversial one even today with Jerry Falwell and others like Jim Dobson assuming an extreme right position. My church has repeatedly said that it loves the sinner but hates the sin, yet it has become so judgmental that no gay would ever feel loved there. I search for the answer to the dilemma still.

Another spiritual problem arose in the month of December in 1992 as I was preparing to say good-bye to Mama. She had been diagnosed with chronic lymphatic leukemia back in 1980, and I felt like her time was short. She had been falling, losing weight, and not eating. In the early morning hours, as I tossed to and fro in my bed at home with insomnia, I had a flashback of being sexually abused by one of our distant relatives.

Again, the sights and sounds from my memory (I didn't think it was a dream) made the conclusion inevitable. I was three, and he was abusing me. Where was my Mama? Why was she not there to protect me? Could this be true, or was I just dreaming after all? I determined to ask her some questions when I flew out to Seattle. One night during my visit, I asked, "Could Tull have sexually abused me?" Her answer confirmed what I already knew, yet it stunned me in another way.

"Yeah, he probably did. One time I got up on his lap, and he put his hand up under my dress. I just jumped down and told him never to do that again," she said.

I was shocked that she took the issue of sexual abuse with me so lightly. I've spent a lot of time in recent years thinking about other children who are also abused. "Why does God allow these types of abuse with innocent children?" I've wondered.

I've also found myself questioning the position of women as interpreted by my Southern Baptist denomination. Recently, the convention voted that women should "graciously submit" to their husbands, creating another firestorm of controversy. I've always had trouble with the idea that women should be docile responders—after all, my own mother was an independent single parent, and it was her example that I saw day-to-day as I grew up. She was certainly never submissive about her opinions. Why should a woman not speak in the church (in other words, teach men in a Sunday school class or even be a pastor if she believes pastoring or teaching is her spiritual gift)? I also started thinking a lot about the presentation of women in the Bible. If Solomon were the wisest man in the world at the time in which he lived, why did he have a thousand wives and concubines? What about their sexual and emotional needs? Assuming he slept with one a night for all of his life, practically, her number would come up for sex just once every three years. How could marriage be fulfilling for her?

I looked around to see true Christian examples and could find few in the church. Just about the time one would convince me that he was a true Christian, he'd divorce his wife of twenty-five years for a sweet young thing instead, all the while promoting family values and condemning Bill Clinton for his behavior.

In addition to these religious and family issues, I had also lost two close friends to death far before their time. One was barely fifty years old and one in her early forties. I sat by both of their hospital beds—comforting, bearing gifts, cheering them on through Scripture verses—but having to struggle myself with anger about their upcoming early deaths.

In my current position as chair now of the English department, I think I've just grown tired and unable to cope any more with the same optimistic spirit I've always had in spite of my childhood trauma. I still have more than ten years to teach though and long for a sense of community, love, and acceptance where I am. Occasionally, I write a column for the school newspaper expressing an opinion that those who are marginalized be accepted with love instead of hate, with tolerance instead of intolerance, with joy rather than with sorrow. When I do, I'm usually criticized for having no sense of true theology and interpretation of Scripture.

I try to look beyond my microcosmic world but find no solace even in the business world, which is so busy merging and downsizing that the common, hardworking person is forgotten.

My own husband has gotten downsized after spending twenty-six years and countless days, weeks, and hours in overtime working for a "caring hospital in a caring community." He was fifty-seven at the time, and his early retirement will last us just five years before it ends when he's 62. After that, he gets Social Security only.

These are grave thoughts, I think as I stand at Mama's grave, longing to return to a sense of innocence and awe of the world. Perhaps, though, it never was possible to have it since I agree with Matthew Arnold's view of the world in his classic poem "Dover Beach":

> . . .for the world which seems
>> To life before us like a land of dreams,
>> So various, so beautiful, so new,
>> Hath really neither joy, nor love, nor light,
>> Nor certitude, nor peace, nor help for pain;
>> And we are here as on a darkling plain
>> Swept with confused alarms of struggle and flight,
>> Where ignorant armies clash by night.

Struggling and fleeing—is that what I'm doing by my pursuit of the Skagway connection? Do I really feel that I can have any more of a coherent, logical view of the world than Mama does in Washington Memorial Gardens on a Seattle-gray day? Even though I know and agree still with the apostle Paul in I Corinthians 13 that we all "see in a mirror, dimly" while we are on this earth, I still long to know more. I must know more in order to go forward. I glance once more at the praying hands statue and walk to the car, resigned.

Chapter Four
The Summer of Thai Chai

"Do you want that cold or warm?" the owner of the Norland General Store near Port Hadlock, Washington, asks me as
Garlan and I stopped by for a latte (the latest "hot" drink is a
Thai Chai, which is made of black tea, honey, ginger, and frothed
milk) and a cold drink. We stroll through the aisles, remembering other general stores from our childhood. While he
remembers the ones in the Ozarks around Jay, Oklahoma, and
Gentry, Arkansas, where he drank Grapettes and ate Moon Pies,
I remember the one in Webb, Mississippi. Dewey, my great
uncle and Elise's husband (Mam's half sister whose middle
name I carry), owned a general store for a while before he had
a heart attack and died while he was in his early forties.

The store was on the main street of town and was long
and narrow in the interior. Typically, the old men gathered
either in front on the two benches on either side of the door or
in the inside on the benches by the wood stove if the weather
was cool. All subjects, especially state politics and the state of
the cotton crop, were discussed. It might as well have been the
one described in Eatonville, Florida, in one of Zora Neale
Hurston's novels.

I was living with Elise and Dewey and, again, was just
three going on four in the summer of 1948. Since the days were
so extremely humid and hot, no one bothered to dress me in

anything but panties only throughout the day whether I was inside or outside. I had blond, curly ringlets like Shirley Temple's (all mothers' idea of a Hollywood angel), which fell naturally around the sides of my face. I'm sure I inherited the naturally curly hair from Daddy since one of his nicknames was Curly. Judy was tall for her age and lanky. She had dark, straight hair, which she usually wore in pigtails, and had a lot of freckles caused by the Mississippi summer heat. Judy and I played for hours on Elise's front porch or in the front yard of the house surrounded by massive pecan trees.

Evidently, Mama and Daddy were having more of their hard times together and apart, so we stayed there a lot. Dewey and Elise's two children, Betty and Robert, were already teenagers, and I guess both Dewey and Elise decided at this time they wanted to care for another young child. After all, I was Elise's namesake. Dewey offered to adopt me.

"Frances, Elise and I can give Lisa a heck of a lot better care than you can. You and Mike live such crazy lives that she'd be more settled here."

"What about Judy?" Mama asked as she thought about their offer. "What would I do about Judy?"

"We can only take Lisa," Dewey replied.

Mama had come there to ask to borrow money from Dewey in order to tide us over for a little while longer. She hadn't even considered the possibility that they'd want one of her girls. She had brought her silverware with her in a wooden chest for collateral since she knew Dewey always looked at everything as a business proposition. One cultural aspect of the South that I've always been surprised by is that, no matter how poor people are, they always seem to own a good set of china and silverware. I recently asked Elise (who was about to celebrate her ninetieth birthday) where Mama got the silverware.

"It was a gift from your daddy," she replied.

That day as a child I sat in my panties in the breakfast area—alone with the silverware chest while the grown-ups talked about my fate. Would it be me, or the silverware, or perhaps both that would be collateral for the loan Mama was about to receive? I had a Buffalo nickel in my hand (probably a gift from Daddy Tull); I took it and began to carve on the chest, making deep marks upon it that would never be erased.

Dewey had already been acting like a daddy to Judy and me anyway. Elise was always having a lot of family over to eat since she was an excellent cook. While she had a large dining room and a good number of chairs both there and in the breakfast area, the overflow crowd, consisting of the sacrificial hosts and the children, always had to go to the back porch for their meal. That was where I sat one day—refusing to eat my green peas.

"Martha Elise," Dewey ordered, "You WILL sit here until you eat all these peas."

I pouted and evidently sat for hours at the table all alone until he gave up the battle. My own Daddy was far too easy-going to ever insist upon such a silly thing.

I hoped Mama wouldn't give me away. I didn't want to be separated from Judy, who was more like a Mama to me than my real Mama. It was she who took care of me from the beginning it seemed, even though sometimes bad things happened when she wasn't real careful in her job as a mama. For example, I was on Elise's high bed in one of her bedrooms when I was just eighteen months old, and Mama told Judy to watch me while she went out of the room for awhile. Eighteen-month-olds can be very fast, and I fell off the bed and broke my collarbone. In 1945, the doctors treated this injury by putting on a brace that caused abrasions on my skin that chaffed and bled. Mama would put cotton under the brace to help as I scratched, pouted, and whined constantly about the uncomfortable brace.

While I'm sure it was tempting for Mama to let Elise and Dewey adopt me, she said no eventually. I think I know what changed her mind, but then I would only be speculating.

Speculating—that's what I do a lot these days. The Norland General Store, which has the look and feel of the general stores from our childhood, with the exception of the new espresso bar, is located halfway home to the north wind—in the Olympic Peninsula forty miles northwest of Seattle.

My initial plan was to travel to Skagway to confront the giants of childhood and religion for a full seven months. I thought that would be about right since seven represents completeness in the Bible—the world was created in seven days.

I set about trying to rent someplace out in Alaska but found that since it's a tourist town, housing is next to impossible during the summer months. Normally there are just a mere seven hundred or so year-round residents, but the number swells to close to 700,000 with the summer visitors and the cruise ship passengers who come in for the day to shop, ride the White Pass & Yukon Railway, or take tours of the spectacular scenery.

Kimberly got on the Internet and found us a one-hundred-year-old house here in Port Hadlock to rent for the summer, and Cindy in Skagway promised to rent us her place through the fall. The house here is a bit musty but, as the ad promised, is comfortably furnished with antiques, including a piano. Kathy and Ted, the owners, have a sailing business which they run every summer from the Orcas Islands. Therefore, the house is ours from June 15 to September 15, at which time we'll take a ferry from Port Angeles, just forty miles from here to Victoria, B.C., and then drive up Vancouver Island to Port Hardy. At Port Hardy, we'll take a ferry up through the Inside Passage to Prince Rupert, which will put us on the Alaskan and Klondike Highways into Skagway. I'll feel like Odysseus going from one island or mainland to another—by ferry, car, train and plane, though, for my modern odyssey.

The ferry ad promises that the journey will take us "through calm inlets, evergreen-covered islands and majestic coastal mountains." The great scenery is supposed to remind us that we're part of something larger. I hope so. I need that reassurance.

In the meantime, we take advantage of the local activities. I try to relax from the busyness of academic life. The tenseness in my neck started to dissipate the farther west I went just six weeks ago now. Our house is complete with outdoor cats, Kate and Allie, plus at least two other neighboring kitties, Chichka and an unidentified black one. In addition, at least three raccoons and several dogs come up the stairs and onto the front porch for regular snacks of cat food. The cushions that I bought at Wal-Mart for the wicker furniture are covered with cat hair, but I just turn them over when I go out to sit.

Like most Southern women, I consider the front porch to be far more than just a place for daydreaming. In the South, it's where one takes a Coke or a gigantic glass of iced tea and sits for hours with friends—or alone—to work out the dilemmas of life. Now I settle into a wicker chair with my Thai Chai from the general store. Garlan's not much of a porch sitter since he's from Kansas with its continual hot winds (so special in the summertime as one of the lines from the film *The Presidio* reminded us, so more often than not, I'm left alone with my thoughts and my turmoil).

From our summer porch, I can see a glimpse of the water beyond the trees, and on the clearest of days here in the Northwest, I can see the snow-peaked mountains beyond. The sky is almost that shade of country blue that was popular in the 1980's, but the water appears more aqua than blue. The trees are so much bigger here on the edge of the American rain forest it seems (no doubt because of all that constant rain that serves as a moisturizer to my dry skin); they obscure the vision, and I wish someone could cut some of the brush back across the way so that I could see more clearly.

Mama would have loved this place since she loved the saltwater and the ocean (or gulf or bay or inlet). She always said she felt like she had "died and gone to heaven" when she could be around the water and a beach, and to put a mountain in the scene would be like Mount Olympus (the home of the Greek gods as well as the highest peak in the nearby Olympic National Park) to her. She rarely got scenes like this while living in the Mississippi Delta, that's for sure.

At times she was more like Daddy than Judy and I were. She would become so restless that she'd quit her current job in Greenville at one of the restaurants and just take off to the Gulf Coast in Mississippi. The first time she did this I was ten, and Judy was fourteen. The problem was always money. How would we be able to afford to do it? One of her customers was an old Jewish man whose name was Mr. Levi. I remember his coming over to the apartment late one night and taking out a hundred dollar bill from his wallet, which he gave to Mama. I had never seen one before, so I was fascinated.

"I'll pay you back every penny, Mr. Levi. I'll get a job on the coast and pay you back in installments," Mama promised.

"Honey, you can begin to pay me back now," Mr. Levi replied as he slithered over toward Mama and tried to kiss her on the lips.

I was shocked, since I never thought Mama kissed any-one but us lightly on the lips as she said good-bye to Judy and me every day when she went to work. Mama was able to divert his kiss this time and quickly usher him outside the door.

"That old goat," she said as she closed the door. "Why did he think I'd want anything but a loan from him?"

As an adult now, again I marvel at Mama's naiveté.

Our first experience on the coast led us to a house right on the beach in Gulfport. Once again, Mama used her expertise in talking to the landlady and finding the best place she could afford for us. This time her name was Mrs. Estes, and I guess, as the other landladies of the past had done, she felt sorry for us. Our apartment was upstairs with a kitchen the size of a small closet maybe. There were two other rooms—a living room and a bedroom, which were quite spacious, along with a small bath-room.

Judy and I spent our days out on the pier, crab fishing and swimming. Neither one of us liked the thought of throwing live crabs into boiling water to enjoy the savage sport of then eating them, so we just sold them at the end of the day to the highest bidder (usually a good number of crabs—fifteen or twenty—went for $1). We thought the money was exceptionally good.

Mama would get a job at whatever restaurant she could. It was always tourist season in the summer, so it was easy for her. David, Elise's youngest child who came along after Mama refused to let her and Dewey adopt me when I was three, came down to visit us every summer. He was like our brother since Betty Jean and Robert, his older siblings, were grown already. He and I got into a lot of fights usually, since I was just three years older than he and thought I could boss him around as I was bossed around by Judy. My fingernails were always long, and he still remembers his painful scratches even today and tells his children how mean I was back then. Dewey had died when David was just five, so Elisc had to raise him alone too like Mama was raising us. Unlike me, who never appreciated what a fine waitress our Mama was, David remembers admiring her since she could fill both arms full of plates and deliver them safely and hot to her customers with seemingly little effort.

"What time are we eating?" Garlan calls from the house and disturbs my reverie. He's been working inside back at the desk on our bills. I've started to identify more and more with Madame Bovary lately. It seems that, since Garlan's downsizing, we think about money a lot more. In order to get enough rent money for the trip this summer and fall, we sold two cars at Two State Used Cars just over the Oklahoma line. I've taken a lot of extra jobs this past year too—May term, two adult education classes, and a North Central consultant-evaluator's chair role—to help finance this trip "to the home of the north wind," and I'm pulling out my gold card far more than I wanted to.

No one seems to understand the depth of my obsession but me. They ask me, "Why can't you discover the answers to life's big questions at home?" At this point I can't provide them with any definitive answer. I've just been "lured," as the slutty character in *Bull Durham* says to explain her obsession with men, and a lot of them.

This is the summer of the Thai Chai I tell myself, on the porch with the cats and occasionally the raccoon. The home to the north wind will be for the fall. I wonder why women like me won't take no for an answer when a trip like this obviously isn't economically feasible. I wonder why I'm so driven.

I sit on my porch, thinking these thoughts, drinking Chai, knowing its healthy, healing benefits are being recommended all over by everyone. I'm beginning to suspect that Lake Wobegon isn't the only place where all the women are strong and the children are above average. I'll once again "go through the drawers" of Mam's, yet another time, as I sift through the scrapbook of memorabilia—hoping to leave the chaff behind and come away with the pure white residue of meaning.

Chapter Five
Thursday Afternoons at the Rose

"I've always lived in a world of reality rather than illusion," I think to myself as Garlan and I enter into the world of the Rose. It has taken us several weeks here in the Port Townsend, Washington area, to discover the theater. We had seen the movie marquees and knew we wanted to see a film there while we were in our summer limbo before Skagway, but we weren't particularly tempted by the movie offerings at first.

We now walk into the foyer of the ancient theater, which houses two screens, and place the stubs of our tickets into the antique-looking container marked "ticket stubs." The aroma of the popcorn (as it usually does) beckons us there first, and we glance at the sign above the counter, which promises us that we'll be eating a large bag of healthy popcorn since it's cooked in canola oil, rather than dastardly coconut oil. We are surprised that the prices are so reasonable. Since we're on a tight budget (for the past year or so), we're used to selecting the smallest sized bag, a minuscule offering at $3.50 or $4.00. Here we can get a large bag for $3.00. We're still not used to the hot beverages available here in Washington at the movie theater, like hot teas and cappuccinos, so we forgo those for our usual choice—diet Pepsi (Coke is almost non-existent in the Northwest, it seems, and its absence presents quite a trauma to us Southerners). We've arrived thirty minutes early and pay matinee prices, which saves us $2.00.

We feel we've returned to the world of the 1950s, the world where we were first introduced to Saturday newsreels, cartoons before the movie, trailers, and the featured attraction. The theater is spotless, unlike our usual experience of traipsing through tons of stickiness on the floor in a Southern theater. The floors are wood, and the wallpaper has Victorian flowers, which repeat the message in a border throughout the interior of the theater, "the rose in the wilderness." I wonder if the reference is to Isaiah 35:1, "The wilderness and the wasteland shall be glad for them. And the desert shall rejoice and blossom as the rose." I feel sure it is. In the center of the screen, we also see reminders of days of yore with the words "Rosebud Cinema" taking us back, along with Orson Wells, to the memories of his childhood sled in *Citizen Kane*. The quiz questions follow, but this time, instead of asking the usual questions about which Tom Cruise film featured him as a pilot, we are challenged with questions from the nostalgic days of Hollywood where the stars were big (really big, as Ed Sullivan might have said) and under contract to the major studios.

Before the feature begins, I slip away to the bathroom downstairs, and a poster greets me, featuring a movie star from the past who beckons me to enter. The mirror above the sink is starlike with makeup mirrors above and Marilyn Monroe decoupaged in its center. Thousands of other stars (it seems) appear around the mirror's border, reminding me of their power and presence from the past.

The power of films, and the awe of being transported into a similar but different world, has always been with me. Mama was a movie aficionado (as well as a popcorn aficionado). When we couldn't afford to go to the movie in Greenville, Mama would send Judy and me into the lobby for a ten cent bag of butter-flavored, fragrant popcorn, which Mama would then eat as we walked back to our apartment at 633 Central, not too far from downtown.

One of my earliest memories of when we were still a family was going to the movies with Mama, Daddy, and Judy. Daddy would thrust me up onto his knees when the cartoon started and say, "Little widget, it's time for the cartoons!" I'm not sure where he got that nickname' or others that he would later call me, like "Mama's little angel" (tongue-in-cheek, I now know). Unfortunately though, by three, I was already a serious child and found little enough to smile about and certainly not ever enough to laugh about. The antics of Bugs Bunny, Casper, the Friendly Ghost, Tweetty Bird, or the Roadrunner were not of the slightest interest to me. They were just silly and unreal to me. I purposely would sit sullenly on Daddy's lap and refuse even to smile.

What I did thrill to though were the dramas, often re-released several years after their initial debuts. *Gone With the Wind* was especially powerful as Scarlett swore that she'd never, ever be hungry again (just before the intermission when we had all gotten tremendously hungry ourselves and went for snacks immediately after her famous lines were uttered). Or how about *Showboat* with Howard Keel and Paul Robeson singing every few minutes on the dock about their sad plights and their longing for "Ol' Man River." It became pure ecstasy to me. The sadder the lives portrayed in the film, the happier I became. My own lot somehow didn't seem too much to bear. Others had it just as hard as I (at least on screen).

I don't think a lot has changed for me in that regard. I still prefer dramas over comedy any day. At the Rose, the owner appears shortly before each film and speaks directly to the audience with a small note card for reminders of his message. He speaks of the film, its idea, its stars, and its director; and he gives funny little stories about the making of the piece. It's obvious that he loves and gets a lot of energy by what he's doing; I envy him.

As we've watched the films of the last two weeks at the Rose, we've seen the plight of children portrayed in both. One was a Harvey Keitel piece written and directed by a Viet namese, Tony Bui. The other was a Franco Zeffirelli film based on his memoirs in Italy before World War II. Both presented children who were unwanted and who struggled to survive. Bui showed one of his child protagonists losing his wooden case filled with cigarettes and cheap watches, which he sells to the tourists in Saigon. Because the child doesn't have the burden of being an adult now, he can be free to be who he is, at least temporarily. He stoops by the gutter on one of those monsoon nights and fashions a boat out of cardboard—playing, like the child he is, in the water. When he recovers his case, adulthood and survival again become the central issue for him. The Zeffirelli film showed a child whose mother is dead and whose father didn't want him because he would interfere with the father's new marriage.

Even though fifty years of movie-going have come and gone with me, I can still be had by the dramas. "You complete me," says Jerry Maguire to his wife near the end of the film. "Stop, you had me when you said 'Hello,'" replies Dorothy. *The Rose* has me for the next six weeks—hands down. *The Rose* is an experience, not just a movie; its view of reality is powerful.

Chapter Six
Treasures of Tradition

Garlan and I walk into First Presbyterian Church, located in the uptown area of Port Townsend, Washington. Old traditions die hard, it seems. Some on a seven-month sabbatical might choose to avoid church attendance and could even convince themselves that they had a legitimate reason to do so. We're so used to the Sunday morning routine though, after all these years, that it seems a natural act to us to seek out a church —even a temporary one. We notice the interim pastor's name is Samuel Adams, which seems quite appropriate since all of the surrounding streets in the Uptown area are named for United States presidents—Franklin, Jefferson, Adams, Lincoln, and so on. We wonder if the pastor had to meet an additional criterion of sounding presidential as well before he was hired.

We've chosen the Presbyterian denomination and this particular church for several reasons. It's located in a beautiful part of the town overlooking the water of the Strait of Juan de Fuca, and the building was likely constructed in the late 1800s in this town that bills itself as a Victorian seaport. There aren't many Southern Baptist churches readily available here, although we do know there's one on Discovery Road (great street name for a church, I'd say). There's also some history of Presbyterian influences in our family from the past.

Mama and Daddy were married by a Presbyterian min-

ister in 1937, Mam attended the Presbyterian church in Skagway when she stayed for several weeks with Pop during the war,
and I went to a Presbyterian kindergarten. Father Noonan was
the priest there, and I remember him as a kindly man who one
day sat on the steps with me while I cried for Mama. She always
walked several blocks from our apartment on Central Street to
pick me up after the morning session ended. This particular day,
however, she was nowhere in sight when I came bounding out of
the side door of the education building and into the welcoming
sunlight. I was brave for a while, but when all of my classmates
had gone away with their respective mothers, I didn't know what
else to do but to sit down and cry. Father Noonan might have
heard me, since I've never cried undramatically. I figure, if one
is unhappy, she has every right, and even obligation, to make
sure someone else in the world knows of her plight.

He sat beside me and held my hand. "Elise," he said gently, "I'm sure your Mama will be here soon. She hasn't forgotten you." Elise, as he called me, still sounded a bit strange
to me (after all, that was my aunt for whom I was named), but
it was easier just to let the teachers call me that through the
years, rather than lamely try to explain that Mama called me
Lisa as a nickname in spite of the fact that my given name was
Martha Elise.

After what seemed like an incredible amount of time, we
noticed Mama as she came limping up the sidewalk. "Where've
you been? I didn't know where you were!" I went running to

her, crying and hugging her.

It turns out that she had dropped the Dutch oven on her toe back at the apartment and had been doing more crying than I and wondering how she was ever going to walk several blocks to the Presbyterian church and pick me up. We were able to limp home together, me with my wounded feelings of another near abandonment and her with a real injury. I still don't know how she was able to get her waitress shoes on that day and go to work for her split shift. Some fifty years later it's as if the incident just happened in my mind.

As we slip into a pew at the Port Townsend church, I notice that the front of the auditorium has a large cartoon drawing showing a picture of a biblical village with two camels (both of whom seemed to be wearing red lipstick) on the sides. I read the church bulletin, which announces that Bible school for the children has been a great success.

As the sermon begins, Pastor Adams speaks of the treasures of tradition, which must and should be taught to the children. The text of his sermon is found in Matthew 13, where Jesus teaches the principles of the heart to His disciples by using parables. There are six, including the parable of the mustard seed, the leavening for the bread, and the seeking of that which is lost. After he completes a summary of each, he asks the congregation, "Do you understand the parables?"

I begin to squirm and feel as I did as a child when the teacher asked which of the servants should be rewarded—the one who had been given five talents, or ten talents, or one. I'm afraid to give the wrong answer again even at age fifty-four. The congregation is also hesitant to respond until an ancient lady with white hair behind us calls out, "Yes." The answer parallels the disciples' answer when Jesus asked them the same question. As for myself, I'm not so sure I do understand the parables still. I know Jesus used them to help clarify the difficult theological issues. I tell myself that I have the advantage of fifty years within the church, unlike the disciples who had a mere three years with Jesus to learn all there was to know. I have the advantage of the written Word and have sat under the teaching of many wonderful pastors who explained the Word so beautifully. Yet I sit in my pew, realizing that my faith is more of an emotional faith rather than an intellectual one. I still see through the mirror perhaps just as darkly as I always have.

I begin to remember my own experiences in Vacation Bible school. Judy and I always went to Mam and Pop's house immediately after the school year ended in Greenville in May. Bible school would begin the Monday after our school year ended. We yearned to be able to sleep late (not "in"—only Yankees say that), but Mam would come to our bedroom door about six o'clock announcing the imminent approach of Bible school at the First Baptist Church of Tutwiler where they lived.

"Ya'll get up. Today's the first day of Bible school."

Was this yet another ploy—like checking the mail each day or napping for two hours just to provide some free time for her while Pop was working on the railroad? I felt sure it was, but once we were out of bed, I looked forward to the next two weeks. I loved the pageantry of it all—marching down the center aisle of the little church for the opening ceremony and listening to the announcements each morning. The preparation, and announcement of it to the townspeople in Tutwiler, began with a kids' parade through town, where we decorated our bicycles (the old, blue one was still rideable, though not pretty) with crepe paper—all shades of the rainbow. Little kids also had their red wagons and sat in the center of them, while their older siblings pulled them slowly over the gooey blacktopped streets in the Mississippi heat. Even the neighborhood dogs did not escape the parade and followed their masters with crepe paper bows around their necks.

Bible schools always began promptly at 8 a.m., and Mam fed us her usual big breakfast of burned bacon, eggs fried hard (doctors today are now saying this is a good choice once again, although Judy and I would have preferred over-easy if given an opportunity to choose), grits with tons of real butter oozing onto the plate, and biscuits and molasses.

I can hear the pianist, now playing, "Onward Christian Soldiers" as we marched in. I wanted to be one of the three flag bearers every day, but unfortunately, the teachers insisted that all the children be given an opportunity during the two-week period. We would pledge allegiance to all three—the United States flag, the Christian flag, and the Bible—every morning,

"I pledge allegiance to the Bible, God's holy Word, and will make it a lamp unto my feet and a light unto my path, and will hide its words in my heart that I might not sin against God."

Announcement time was even better and often held the promise of something quite exciting for me. Often the pastor would promise a tangible reward to the first boy and first girl, for example, who would learn an entire chapter in the Old Testament. Even today I see the gigantic Baby Ruth candy bar being held up as a promise to the first ones who would memorize Psalms 24.

"Oh, shucks," I'd think to myself, "Why not Chapter 23? I already know that one." On this occasion, I flipped immediately in my Bible and noticed that it was not too long but contained the word "Selah" for no apparent reason after every verse. I set about my task while the announcements were continuing. Back then I could memorize very fast and delighted in winning every contest. I even learned the books of the Bible (both Old and New) and said them rapidly before the whole congregation (mispronouncing many of them, I'm sure). I'm not sure where I got my extremely competitive spirit since Mama, Daddy, and Judy didn't seem to have one.

The next day just Billy Bruister and I had learned all of Psalm 24. I rattled mine off rapidly (as usual) before the whole crowd, totally unaware of any meaning connected to the words—but a winner anyway of the giant Baby Ruth. I could already taste its sweet chocolate and peanuts gooey with caramel. Billy, however, had a harder time. He struggled and struggled with the words until all of us thought we'd never get beyond the announcements for the second morning and would just have to go home when the eleven o'clock bell range for dismissal. When the final "Selah" was uttered, we were all rejoicing to God.

After the announcements, we broke up into our smaller groups based on age and had the Bible story for the day. It usually lasted about an hour, and I, along with the other fellow sufferers in the Word, was thrilled when the bell rang announcing refreshment time around 10 a.m. We all knew what the snacks would be—KoolAid and donated cookies from the Mamas (and Mams) of the neighborhood. They were always served outside (certainly for a purpose because by the end of our fifteen-minute break, several of the kids had spilled theirs on the sidewalk). The day would already be sweltering, even in late May, by 10 a.m., with the usual combination of heat and humidity.

The last lesson of the day would always center on missions either at home or in a foreign country. I remember one day Miss Polly was trying to get us to hear the call of God early by listening to God Who would call us to a ministry just as certainly as He called Samuel when he was living with old Eli. She, like Jesus in the parables in Matthew 13, used an example to help us understand.

"Ya'll know Billy Graham, don't you? What does he do?" she inquired of us.

We all raised our hands since Billy Graham was just a

young man back in the early 50s, and we were so impressed in the Southern Baptist Church by his call to evangelism. This time I was certain I knew the answer, but before anybody was chosen to answer, someone else hollered out.

"He goes around preaching the Gospel to everybody all over the world."

"Yes, you're right. When God called him when he was young, God laid a hand on him."

Billy Bruister, though not too sharp, in my opinion, in memorizing Scripture verses for candy, piped up and hollered, "I'd say He laid TWO hands on him."

While I still "see through a glass darkly," I yearn to know more. Today the pastor completes his sermon by admonishing the congregation not to let religion and church attendance become just a "holy habit" or a "page in a book of minutes" but to let our belief and faith be real and vibrant, resulting in care and concern for the needs of others in the community. Perhaps he's right. I do dwell on myself a lot and seem at times to be almost totally self-absorbed. I'll think of these lessons—but another day maybe. As Scarlett says, "Tomorrow is another day." The treasures of tradition do last a lifetime; that I believe.

Chapter Seven
The Haunting at 130 Hadlock Ave.

It's nearing midnight, and I'm luxuriously taking advantage of my relaxed evenings here in Port Hadlock. I find myself tensing slightly, however, as I watch one of the "Midsummer Night's Scream" series on television. This one's entitled *The Haunting at Seacliffe Inn* and stars the familiar actress from St. Elmo's Fire, Allie Sheedy. Her character and her husband have bought a spooky, old house and plan to operate a bed and breakfast, only to find it haunted by ghosts of the past. As is typical in formulaic plots of this type, it becomes a war of ghosts vs. humans, with the stronger of the two usually winning out. While I never fear for the characters' fate, I sometimes wonder about winning over the ghosts (or giants) of my past.

I'm as bad as Scrooge since I've finally decided to confront the ghosts of my Christmas pasts too. I am strangely haunted by the contents within this house and wonder how this amalgamation has occurred. Ted and Kathy's house at 130 Hadlock Ave. is like the characters' house in the movie in that it's one hundred years old. It is evidently featured in the Port Townsend Historical Museum by photograph (although Garlan and I couldn't find it when we took a tour recently and asked three of the museum volunteers to assist us).

Since I was a child, I've always been a nut for riding down the road in a car and looking into the lighted houses on the side of the road as the light of day fades into darkness. I imagine what it would be like to live in that house. What would my daily life be like? What would I be eating for supper that night? When I became an adult, I tried to analyze this compulsion of searching for a different life, and hopefully a better one. Was it because my early life with Mama and Daddy was so difficult? After all, I lived in many different home environments through the early years—with the four of us as a family, with Elise and Dewey, with Mother and Judy only, with Mam for the five years I was in high school, and with Mama and her new husband for a short time. Or was it simply evidence of a creative mind?

Now that I have had the opportunity to live someone else's life, using their dishes, their towels, and their linens for a three-month period, I'm comforted by the familiarity I feel in doing so. The kitchen is wonderful, a farm kitchen with a large oval table and a separate wooden cupboard. The sink is old with no disposal and no dishwasher. My mind goes back to Mam's kitchen when she and Pop bought their first house in Tutwiler. Since he worked for the bulk of his career for the Illinois Central Railroad, they had always lived in section houses provided by the company. When he retired early because of his failing health, however, it became necessary for them to buy a home. Today I think our young married couples could hardly imagine not buying a home until retirement.

Mam insisted that the renovation of the tiny, white frame house on a corner of Tutwiler's busiest road include the addition of a large kitchen. She rationalized, "I spend all my time in the kitchen. I told Slick it had to be a big one, bigger than any other room in the house. My two great loves are eating and watching TV." So, the kitchen was completed—with Mam's specifications exactly. The pattern of the linoleum floor was a red brick tile-look (most folks couldn't afford to put ceramic tile down). We spent hours in that kitchen as a family. We helped her cook for the large family dinners she would prepare around the holidays; we helped her do the dishes. We talked with one another.

Today at 130 Hadlock Ave. I stare at the same linoleum that was in Mam's kitchen. I'm sure it was a popular choice in the mid-50s in a lot of American households. I also stare at the same make and model refrigerator Garlan and I had in the early 70s. Like Mam's kitchen, which had a swinging door separating it from the dining room (she wanted it in order to keep the hot temperatures out of the main house in the summer), Kathy's kitchen is separate from the living room. Garlan and I have eaten practically every meal in this country kitchen, not in front of the TV, as we do at our home in Siloam Springs, Arkansas, where we live today, but across from each other at the oval table. Robert Frost's character in his famous poem said, "Good fences make good neighbors." I say, "Good kitchens make good families." We talk to one another again.

The main room of the house has an antique flowered sofa with lumpy cushions that sit at an angle from a wood burning fireplace, not the usual enclosed one but one with glass in the front, allowing viewers to watch the fire as well as feel its encircling heat. It's already been used several times during these cold, Washington mornings. Our house in Tontitown also had a wood stove manufactured by Fireview with a glass front. During the busy years of the early 1980s, as I was working on my doctoral degree, I would sit during holidays immobilized before its hypnotic flames as I tried to relax from the grind of teaching, mothering, writing papers, taking exams, and studying for comprehensives.

The location of our bathroom here is also typical of an old house in that, of course, there was no indoor plumbing for years. When a bathroom was added, it always seemed to be located on the back porch, which was simply framed in. The plumbing would be near the kitchen. Mam and Pop's last section house had a bathroom in the back as well, once more a converted porch. I used to dread those cold morning visits to the bathroom around the holidays since the floors would inevitably be freezing and the bathroom drafty.

The item of furniture I noticed when I came into Kathy's house for the first time was a large, round wooden coffee table. Garlan and I have one now in our garage at home, and it was the place where our daughter, Kimberly, learned to walk. We remember when Neil Armstrong walked on the moon for the first time ever for an American (or anyone else) in July of 1969. We were students at the University of Mississippi, and like practically everyone else in America, had gotten up to see the event live. Kimberly has always been a morning child, a morning glory, and wanted to be with us as well. We shivered when we heard Neil's words, "This is one small step for man, one giant leap for mankind." Kimberly was in her pajamas, walking around the coffee table, repeatedly practicing those steps that would eventually move her, independent of us, into the larger world around her.

The small Hummel clock in Kathy's bedroom is like the two we have at home. We bought them on one of our trips to Estes Park, Colorado, years ago. The books on her bookshelf are the same I have on mine. The ghosts of the past are here with me, it seems. I really don't live a different life in someone else's house after all.

As I turn the clicker for the television off, and the movie fades into the background, I'm happy for the characters because they were victorious over the ghosts who were haunting them. I'm not quite ready for bed yet. The moon is full tonight, and the meteorologists have said there will be a partial eclipse around 4:30 a.m., which we will be able to view from the northwest area of the Pacific. I know that I'll go to bed before that, but I go to the back office and look out onto the horizon and admire the moon. "I see the moon; the moon sees me," I think of one of my childhood chants. I also remember Warren and Mary in Frost's poem "The Death of the Hired Man," as they sit on the porch steps and ponder what to do with Silas, who has come home (the only home he knew) to die.

I pick up Kimberly's unpublished novel entitled *Unpacking*

(whose title seems curiously appropriate for my odyssey as well these seven months). I marvel at her ability to create 245 separate and complete stories, and I love her idea of linking them together by taking the last line of each and making it the first line of the next. It seems to so connect us with the rest of humanity. After all, I think to myself, it's entirely conceivable to me that if someone is ending a conversation with one of Kimberly's lines, "Scars scare people away," that a person in some other part of the universe could possibly be beginning a conversation with the same line.

I've always enjoyed reading Kimberly's and Chris's creative writing, but I'm disconcerted by the presentation of the mother characters, who are inevitably controlling and manipulative. I tell myself, "It's fiction; surely they aren't writing about me." After all, I once made a statement to myself several years ago, "I might have made some mistakes in the past, but the thing I feel I've done well is to be a mother." I realize today though, as I confront the ghosts on this night of the full moon, that I have indeed been far too controlling with them. I wish I could return to that early morning thirty years ago when Neil Armstrong was taking his small step for himself and the giant leap for humanity, and Kimberly was taking her first steps toward eventual independence, that I could return for a second chance at mothering. Today, though, I leave them both in the hands of Him. My job of mothering, whether good or poor, has passed. I love; I advise, but I can't mother anymore.

I look for answers; I search for meaning—alone and with Garlan at the kitchen table. At my recent conference in Denver on the development of Internet courses, I listened to Harold Heie from the Council of Christian Colleges and Universities. The organizers set up a telephone conference, and we sat in a Marriott meeting room and heard him discuss integration of faith and learning. He reminded us that we seek meaning from external sources at times, and we seek meaning from internal ones as well. He believes most people do a combination of both, rather than one or the other. The examples he used are that God gave the Bible (an external source of truth and meaning), but He also gave humans the ability to analyze and interpret and develop meaning (internal; it happens in the brain).

I know that my odyssey and pursuit of the Skagway connection will be both as well. I roam the country from Arkansas to Oklahoma to Kansas to Colorado to Utah to Oregon to Washington—like Odysseus seeking the next giant (or ghost) like Polyphemous to overcome, or seeking the glorious quest of adventure only, but I also roam within my mind and my memories seeking to be enlightened. I'm like the Ulysses (Odysseus' Roman name) from Tennyson's poem, I go both without and within, "To strive, to seek, to find, and not to yield."

Chapter Eight
The Secrets of Mother Forest

"This is the forest primeval," I think of Longfellow's words in his poem "Evangeline" about the French Arcadians making their long trek down from the Newfoundland area to settle in the Louisiana bayous. What a journey that must have been back several hundred years ago, I marvel. Though a fictional story of peril and young love, it's based, loosely at least, on the historical event. On this day Garlan and I walk in Olympic National Park with the naturalist who's accompanying us, along with a family of two parents and four children and another young woman who is videoing the tour for her relatives back home in North Carolina. Along the way, in her animated, enthusiastic manner (even after four years and countless tours with other people), Christie shares with us the "secrets of the forest." We pause every few hundred feet, it seems, to view five-hundred-year old trees, pick up pine cones to see the secrets, and learn of their struggle to survive—and even be respected.

Christie asks each family to tell where they're from and asks us if we have hiked other state and national parks in the area. We mention when it's our turn that Hot Springs National Park is in our state and that our children were junior naturalists at Devil's Den State Park when the program was initiated for kids in the early 1970s. At that time we owned a small Apache forest-green camper that folded out supposedly to sleep six people. The four of us found ourselves extremely cramped, however, on those rainy camping days, during which we had to stay inside, watch our small TV, nap, and play cards. Most of our time on the good weather days was spent, of course, following the set of specifications necessary for Kimberly and Chris to earn their certificates. Those specifications included taking all the hikes in the park, up hillsides, down and around the bluffs, into the Devil's Ice Box, and through Lee Creek. I sometimes sort through their items from childhood, and I find those certificates. I remember once more the times we had together—and, of course, long for them again.

We pause early on our hike today to Marymere Falls and gaze at a strange configuration of a tree. Christie asks us what we see, and the other mother in the group shouts out, "It's a tree which has grown up on an old log."

Christie says, "Good! What you are seeing here is a nurse log. The new trees must be able to get to the light they need, so what they do is attach themselves to an old log and begin their growth."

I look at the old nurse log, which is entwined with numerous branches and roots of the new tree using it for a host. I think to myself that this is how motherhood is for the majority of us. Our children wrap themselves about us for years, taking the nourishment from us as needed and sucking the nutrients from our bodies (I guess both figuratively and literally for nursing mothers). We gladly grant them power to do so because we know they can't grow; they can't become independent; they can't flourish without it. We allow them to push for the light, knowing full well that we, the nurse logs, will no longer be needed after they reach a certain point of growth.

I remember those stages well with Kimberly and Chris. As babies, they were so anxious to stand on their chubby legs atop my lap and reach above their heads, laughing as if they had already understood the concept of the nurse log. Yet it was always about the age of twelve that I could barely convince them to sit in my lap any longer. Their pre-adolescent arms and legs were gangly, but they were able to wrap themselves about me for a short moment before they wanted to be released to the outside world of softball with their friends in our yard in Tontitown. We mothers, on the other hand, seem to become a bit tired and lose our energy as they begin to flourish. Is this what the Bible means when it says in John 3:30, "He must increase, but I must decrease"? We are like the tree in Shel Silverstein's classic children's book, *The Giving Tree,* who gives and gives until there's nothing left for herself. "Does she give too much?" Kimberly asked me recently after reading it.

Our next stop on the hike is to view "Mother Fir," which is one of the oldest trees in the forest where we are by Lake Crescent. Instead of being a nurse log, she towers hundreds of feet into the air by herself and seeks light by growing so tall. While she produces thousands of babies, pine cones, they don't have a chance to become a tree like herself because they are so tiny and have no light. Mother Fir is simply too immense and hogs the light. "Nature, however, has a cure provided by friend squirrel," Christie shares. "She assists Mother Fir by eating the seeds from her pine cones and then depositing them later with her droppings onto other areas of the forest where they can receive the needed light for growth and nourishment to adulthood."

I suppose this is another form of a mother in our society, though a rarer one in my opinion, who, instead of being the vehicle to allow her children growth and independence, has taken all the glory herself. Perhaps she's been so busy with her own needs and her desire for admiration by others that she's neglected to see to the needs of her children. She would hardly be the ideal mother described in Proverbs 31. She's more like Vivi in Rebecca Wells' book, *Divine Secrets of the Ya-Ya Sisterhood,* a mother who's so concerned with drinking and playing cards that she has no time for the children she created. Nevertheless, the children of Mother Fir do find ways to grow up and become independent in spite of the lack of nurturing by their mothers.

The most interesting mother in the forest, to me, is the third example, which we now pause to see. She is the Pacific yew. She's not like the red alder, which had multiple uses for the Native Americans earlier in our history in America. The red Alder's bark was used for even baby diapers (and the lichens also provided an antibacterial for baby's tender skin).

For years though the Pacific yew was called just a "trash tree." It seemed that she had nothing to give to babies or to anyone else. In recent years, however, something wonderful happened. Scientists have discovered a terrific by product available from her—taxol. Taxol is the key ingredient now being widely used for breast cancer and ovarian cancer patients for healing. It is used to make the drug called Tamoxifin. To me, this tree represents the mother in our society who becomes a mother before she's ready to assume the responsibilities of the job. It appears to some in society that she's a trash tree that needs some years of maturing before she can fully give to others her gifts and her healing.

As we approach the last leg of the trip to the falls, we must prepare for the stamina that we need to climb the final one-eighth of a mile, crossing two log bridges and climbing several platforms of steep stairs rising into the mountainside. Garlan and I decide to let the younger, more physically fit climbers go before us. We do manage slowly to climb the final steps, and we are within sight now of Marymere Falls as it cascades down hundreds of feet into a lake. As we see the bank of gigantic, stately trees below, I think of Barbara Walters' question that has caused her much grief and embarrassment in the media world: "If you could be a tree, what kind of tree would it be?" I think now, though, that Barbara wasn't so far off base in her question. Trees do have characteristics of humans as well as the other way around. And, we also agree with Christie; the forest does have many secrets to share.

Chapter Nine
Quasimodo and the Hunchbacks

On the last day of July, Garlan and I sit on the metal chairs in Franklin Court, watching one of the performers adjust her microphone for the upcoming concert/reading in Port Townsend. The town has offered some wonderful cultural experiences for us this summer. We attended a country blues festival when we first arrived on the peninsula at Fort Worden and enjoyed the music on a cool, damp evening in a converted airplane hangar now turned theater. We heard Saffire, the "Uppity Blues Women," and others give a rousing, toe-tapping performance. We heard from the writers conference such greats as Ursula LeGuinn and Alan Cheuse read from their work. Next week we will listen to two classical music performances by both the faculty and the students at the music festival.

This particular performer we are about to watch is a prima donna who barks out orders to the soundmen like a sergeant in a boot camp who's training his recruits. "Look at this!" she screams at the microphone before it drops its head in shame to take this kind of treatment. The soundmen rush to the stage once more and adjust it to just the right height again for her. She's Pat, the accordionist, who will play several tunes for the theme of the performance, which is remembering our heritage, our ancestors, and our origin. "I may not like this," I am thinking to myself.

Soon though I find myself staring at the prima donna in

awe once the show has officially begun, and it's like one of Pat's many other personalities has taken control of her body. She is now personable and likable as she begins to play tunes from the Middle East. Her fellow performer, Richard, evidently a local theater personality, begins to read one of the many stories told by Scheherazade from *The One Thousand and One Nights.* He entertains us with a typical story with its themes of love and compassion. Scheherazade certainly needed to be redundant in this theme in order to teach the king these traits and keep him interested enough in her stories so that he wouldn't kill her as he had his other wives. Richard's rich, deep voice is melodic and soothing. I imagine that he would be wonderful in the local theater productions here, playing all types of roles, from the villain in a melodrama to the Shakespearean hero in Othello.

The third entertainer is a poet whose name is Sandy. She is Jewish, and her poem is about hunchbacks. I'm taken by surprise for a moment because she herself has a back that is curved and humped. She also speaks of a performance coming up in the Uptown Theater, where she will be performing with her group, Quasimodo and the Bell Ringers. Evidently, she plans to read her poetry, and the trio of musicians who will accompany her will perform jazz and blues numbers. I'm still not sure I like this self-deprecating humor, but I vow to reserve my judgment for a few minutes until I hear her piece.

Her poem speaks of a number of Israeli hunchbacks on a pilgrimage who are having their meals in a cafeteria. The imagery she uses is startling as she compares the humps on their backs to a mountain range from afar, and she says it appears as if their journeys have already begun. She makes us laugh with her scenes of the hunchbacks who argue with the cook over the thickness of the blintzes or the price of every item on the ticket. It's hard not to revert, in my mind, to the usual Jewish stereotype of Shylock in *The Merchant of Venice.* She asks near the end of the poem whether the water within the humps of these pilgrims will be able to provide enough nourishment for their own personal journeys through the Sinai Desert.

I begin to think about the truth of her concluding image. While the majority of us do not carry so visible a hump on our backs as does Sandy, we often carry one inside us as large as the naval ship currently docked before our house in Port Hadlock. What we do with the burden within us is very often up to us. It is a conscious decision. We can become totally incapacitated and refuse to go forward because of past inequities and injustices in our lives, or we can move beyond them. We cannot change them; they are just as much a part of who we are as our vital organs. Therefore, we must learn, like Scheherazade's husband, to listen to the stories of love and compassion every night and draw upon those past humps to make humane decisions for the future.

I've always liked the lines from William Gibson's play *The Miracle Worker* where Helen Keller's family begins to pity teacher Annie Sullivan because she and her brother were kept in an asylum with inhumane conditions when she was young. She responds by essentially saying, "It made me strong; it made me who I am."

I suspect all of us have a hump within or a hump without. I pray that we may all, through an overt process of self-discovery, draw upon it for nourishment and not simply use it as an excuse for withering.

By the time the program concludes, we've heard songs and readings from the Middle East to Western Europe to America to Port Townsend. The journey home has taken a mere hour but has given us memorable images and challenged us to each reflect upon our own heritage and the stories we have been given. Was Scheherazade right—are love and compassion the answers that will lead to self-knowledge? I tend to think we'll be back next week to listen for more during our time of limbo.

Chapter Ten
Enigmas—Holding On to My Father's Hand

The phone rang around four o'clock in the afternoon on August 9, 1976. I had just come in from the garden, my back soaked with perspiration and my hands itching from the okra I had just picked. "When will I ever learn to take Garlan's advice and make sure I have my gardening gloves on before I tackle such a task?" I thought. He'd be home for dinner around six, and I still needed to bathe my three-(almost four)-year-old son, Chris, who smelled like a grubby worm after being out in the garden with me. Kimberly was playing with her friend Sarah just two houses down the street, and I would have to call and get her home soon as well. "Oh well, it doesn't matter if dinner isn't exactly on time," I rationalized.

As I said "Hello," I heard raspy weeping on the other end of the line and soon recognized that it was Judy, my sister, who was calling.

"What's wrong," I said feeling a childhood panic that I thought I had overcome years ago, "Is it Mother? Has something happened to Mother?"

"It's Daddy," she cried, "He's dead. They found him beside the road today in Mississippi."

At that point we both burst into loud, dramatic sobs. (I've never been a quiet crier, but Judy can usually let tears drip silently so that no one is aware she's crying. Just hearing her cry so loudly made me even more hysterical.) It took several minutes before we could continue the conversation and begin to make arrangements for us and our families to meet in Mississippi in order to plan the funeral.

As I think about that day now—which was twenty-three years ago today—our reactions in some ways seem overblown because, after all, he was a man we hardly knew. He and Mother had been divorced when we were so young; we knew him only as the man who was forever getting drunk and calling Mother, Judy, or me to send him money again. He had been working up and down the Mississippi River as a deckhand for a number of years before his death. The pattern was as regular as Old Faithful in Yellowstone National Park and totally unlike the meandering river on which he worked.

He would spend six weeks or so working on a barge usually out of St. Louis and stay on it until it reached the Gulf of Mexico at New Orleans. He would stay sober for the time he was on the barge, but payday was as important to him as it was to a sailor who had been on a ship for six months and was arriving at a port city. It hardly took him a night before he was shooting craps, buying everyone drinks in a saloon, and romancing a woman. If he won, he probably took the same action as with my mother while they were together—he would take the money and put it over the bed around them. If she were smart, like my Mother, she likely would hide the money and hope he didn't remember anything the next day. His six weeks' pay would be gone in one night of fun.

I quizzed Judy that August afternoon about the cause of his death. All she knew (and all we ever knew) was that he had been sitting in a bar in the Mississippi Delta town of Hollandale, and some guy had come in shooting up the place. Evidently, he got three bullets in his stomach from a .22 caliber pistol, walked out to Highway 61, told someone he was going to see his kids, and sat down to die. His death certificate says it was a homicide. It seems to us that there must have been more to the story, but we won't know the ending until "we all get to heaven" as the old hymn says.

I do know that Daddy was a seeker like me. I can remember seeing him baptized in the Second Baptist Church in Greenville (it must have been shortly after the church brought over food and presents the Christmas I was three). I can still see him in his white baptismal robe, but I thought he looked uncomfortable in it, and I thought it funny to see his white underwear showing through the wet, clinging gown as he came up from the water. He attended church a few times after that before he went back to his familiar patterns.

One day when we were walking out toward the rear of the auditorium, I lifted my tiny hand, took his in mine, and strolled out beside him. I was horrified when we emerged into the bright sunlight to see that I was holding the wrong man by the hand. I began to cry in embarrassment more than anything else. My Daddy bent down and said, "Little widget, did you get confused? Don't cry, I'll always be here to take your hand."

In spite of his repeated promises to Mother and Judy also that he would be there "to hold our hand," he was soon gone from our lives for the most part, sending money only spasmodically and writing an occasional letter or so. I always wondered what he was searching for and if he ever found it.

As Judy and I planned the funeral, we decided upon the Avent Funeral Home for the location since Mam still lived in her little white house, which she and Pop had bought in the 1950s. She would help make the decisions; we knew Mama couldn't. We would bury him at Odd Fellows (an appropriate name) Cemetery in Greenwood where the Rogers cemetery plot was located. We knew Mam would also host a large dinner after the funeral in her dining room, where we would sit around a table with our two half-brothers (I had never met them before Daddy's death; I just knew they were twins—Billy and Bobby).

The funeral home would be small enough for the few we expected to attend the service, just the immediate family. The day of the funeral arrived, and Judy and I were flabbergasted to see droves of "odd fellows" like Daddy pulling up to the funeral home to attend his funeral. They all knew him as Curly and were a motley crew. All kinds of floozy women with blond and red hair and minidresses came to pay their respects as well as many men who resembled some of the homeless we see on the streets today when we visit New York and Chicago. Their suits (and they did wear them) were as ill-fitting as Raymond's in the movie, *Rainman,* as he and the Tom Cruise character were coming down the escalator in a Las Vegas casino. The mourners had come to pay their respects to the man they called their friend—he had loaned them money, he had bought them drinks, he had married some of the women, and he had lost money to practically all of them. But still they came to say good-bye and to tell Judy and me how much they had all loved him, many sniffing loudly as they hugged our necks.

I had wondered earlier how the police were able to locate us since I knew Daddy was always renting a room, buying new clothes, and then simply leaving everything behind to go up to St. Louis for another trip down the river. He rarely ever had identification on him. Somehow, though, they had found his rented room and discovered a letter I had written him a short time before. They attempted to call me (I was in the garden) and got in touch with Judy first.

Since Judy was living in Mississippi at the time, she was able to go to the room and pick up his personal belongings. When she did, she noticed a Bible on the table beside his bed. It was worn, and when she put it to her nose, there was no doubt that it belonged to him. It smelled of cigarettes and booze. As she flipped through it to see if there were any clues to the egimas of his life, she found a scripture verse in Acts 16. He had underlined the one that says, "Believe on the Lord Jesus Christ and thou shall be saved." We'd like to think

Daddy's search had ended well for him at this point, but only God knows his eternal destiny.

Today we often hear in our churches that the relationship we have with our earthly father has a connection to the relationship we have to our heavenly Father. I realize that I'm also influenced by genes. I search today for answers as fervently as Daddy did. I reach up to take my Father's hand only to discover that it has eluded me. I'm a three-year-old child again, longing for the comfort of the Father.

Chapter Eleven
Searching for the Elusive Light

On this particular Saturday afternoon in downtown Seattle, we enter SAM, the acronym for the Seattle Art Museum, in our quest for the special exhibit on Impressionism. We've waited since June 12 and know that its moment in Seattle will end on August 29—a brief time to catch the light of its beauty. The day is atypical of Seattle's summer in that the clouds above suggest rain. "Surely," I think to myself, "the gods of the weather will smile on this city that almost worships the summer sun. It wants a nice day to celebrate Seafair and to see the renowned Blue Angels fly overhead." After a forty-five minute wait in the winding line outside, we step underneath the legs of a black, towering sculpture of a man, to wait underneath a green tent that will take us into the front door.

We walk into the foyer finally, purchase our four tickets (Kimberly and her partner, Sheri, have accompanied us) and receive a headset, which promises to unveil to us all the secrets of the painters and many of their paintings. For once, the system for viewing has been thought out and revised. In the past at the Metropolitan Museum of Art or the Art Institute of Chicago, I've been spatially confused as I hear the audio directions: "Walk through the arch, look to your immediate left, and up near the top of the adjoining wall. There you will see Degas' painting of …." And these go to a person who has trouble getting home from the dentist we've used for twenty years. By the time I recover enough and decide I truly am standing before the painting being described, the audio description has ended. This time, however, we see a number on each of the featured paintings and are simply directed to punch in the number, followed by the green button. "Aha," I think, "this is a great improvement." We can proceed at our own pace.

We've seen the television ads for the event all summer. At first we were puzzled about what was being advertised. We'd see fruit on a summer table (much like the one we have here in Port Hadlock), but the fruit was beginning to rot slowly; it soon had a fly buzzing around it. Another commercial showed a rather rotund young woman who was posing with a bit of fabric draped about her. She yawned, scratched herself, and generally looked bored. In both of the ads, we then heard the words, "Reality was only the beginning," and realized we'd been hearing spots for the Impressionistic exhibit.

I enjoy art museums and begin to wonder about the age at which a sense of aesthetics attaches itself to us. I cannot remember (and I'm sure I never attended a museum with Mama or Judy as I was growing up). I do remember, however, my own private moment in tuning into the astounding beauty of nature. It happened back during our early days in Greenville at 633 Central. I believe I was about seven (or the early spring of 1952) and Judy was eleven. We simultaneously became ill with a case of red measles. Those who lived during that time remember that the illness was devastating in a number of ways. It could have severe side effects, such as loss of eyesight, if one did not take special precautions. It also lasted a tremendously long time in my opinion—two weeks.

Mama carefully instructed us each day as she left for Azar's in her waitress uniform. "Judy and Lisa, ya'll need to stay in bed, rest and sleep a lot. Whatever you do, you must hear this: Do not—under any circumstances—get out of this dark room. You cannot open the curtains, and you cannot turn on a light. Most of all, you cannot read any of your books. Drink lots of juice and water. Call me if you need anything."

"What do you mean, 'Don't read your books'?" I was thinking. I had a half-finished version of one of the innumerable Bobbsey Twins sagas under my bed.

Still, with all of Mama's admonitions and knowing Judy would call Azar's and tell on me if I dared to disobey, I followed her instructions to a letter. It was not until the end of the second week that both of us grew so bored that we dared sneak out a book and begin to read just a short time every afternoon. We had no television set, so that wasn't a temptation. We were glad though that the radio was there to break the monotony. We got in the middle of the bed we shared, ate oranges, and listened to our favorite programs, "Sergeant Preston of the Yukon," "The Shadow" (our personal favorite, which scared us silly every time it played), and others.

Finally, our days of captivity were over. It was in early

March on a Sunday afternoon when we first made our appearance outside. One of Mama's current boyfriends, Harry, was going to take us on a drive over the Mississippi River (we never owned a car). We'd go over to Lake Village, immediately on the other side of the river from Greenville, and if we were lucky, Harry might stop at Stuckey's (which was a new chain and wildly exciting to us in the '50s) and buy us some candy. I loved the pecan logs the best. I couldn't wait.

As I walked out into the high noon sunshine on that day in 1952, even with sunglasses on, I was astonished by the beauty of nature. The daffodils had magically bloomed overnight, and hundreds of them lined the sidewalk that led to the apartment house where we lived. The grass was as green and vibrant as I've ever seen it to this day, and the sky an azure color. A Kurosawa film would seem dull to these colors. Every sight I saw seemed to be attacking and crushing my brain with its loveliness.

Today, as I walk through the nature scenes of Impressionism inside SAM and view the paintings of Gauguin, Degas, Cassatt, Renoir, Manet, Pissarro, Sisley, and others, I have the same awe of aesthetics that I first developed when I was seven. I laugh to myself as I hear about the controversy first created by this new school of painters in the 1860s and 1870s. "How could anyone have ever believed that these were just raw and unpolished pieces?" I wonder. Yet the critics (who always know everything) believed the paintings to be simply raw, unpolished, and formless.

I perk up as the audio recording tells me of the elusive light which the painters struggled with in their canvases so dominated by its presence. I hear the narrator tell me that the painters essentially had seven minutes to work before the light would change again. "Seven minutes!" I'm surprised and wonder how they could work so fast to capture it.

As we near the end of the exhibit, we view a few paintings of Postimpressionism and learn that the light is not nearly so important in these works. I smile and think, of course, about my frequent statement to my Masterpieces of Literature students every semester, "Now remember, everyone, that every literary period reacts to the previous one."

I guess, in spite of my earlier stance on realism, I still am occasionally a Romantic like the Impressionists. Reality isn't that great. I too look for the elusive light and have come to recognize, like the Impressionists, that we may have brief glimpses of it, but we can never capture it in its fullness. Paul in 1 Corinthians was right, I think; we do see through a glass darkly. The most we can hope for is to have a glimpse of Truth every now and again. And nature still has that power upon me, whether it be through a view of daffodils on a summer day or a walk through a museum. I have to agree with Wordsworth, "To me the meanest flower that blows can give / Thoughts that do often lie too deep for tears."

Before I leave the exhibit, I pause at the museum gift shop to buy a print of Mary Cassatt's piece entitled "The Sisters." The younger one is putting her arm around the other's shoulders. Sisters share a lot, I think, even the measles.

Chapter Twelve
Filming the Makers

It's a lazy August day, and the sun is shining in the Seattle area, making all the natives (and would-be natives like us) want to leave the workplace and the computers for a great Northwestern adventure. Early in the day, one of my former students called to say he was at Whidby Island at his aunt's house for a family reunion. Garlan and I agreed to meet him, his brother Matt, and his other brother Tim for lunch.

This trip was our first on this particular ferry (almost a standard mode of travel for a lot of people here) from Port Townsend to Keystone. On the other side of the island, the low terrain almost reminds us of Dauphin Island out from Mobile (one of our favorite family vacation spots). The houses lazily stand on stilts near the marshy-looking vegetation. The island, in general, seems much more isolated than where we are on the Olympic Peninsula.

After picking the three young men up from their aunt's house, we mosey on back inland a few miles, looking for the little town and the restaurant that had been recommended to us.

"It's called the Doghouse Tavern," instructed the aunt, "But you just ignore that sign and go around to the side of the place where there'll be another sign which says 'Family Restaurant.' It's located in Langley right on First Avenue."

On the road over to Langley, Tim (the going-into-ninth-grade student) mentions that he has read on the Internet about a film that is currently being made in the downtown area. All he knows is that it is about the musician Leonard Cohen (a French-Canadian singer/poet) and that Cameron Diaz is supposed to be there since her boyfriend is starring in it. By a process of elimination, we decide that Cameron's boyfriend for the past few months is Jared Leto, not Matt Dillon anymore, who had kept America laughing in *There's Something About Mary.* We all secretly hope to get a glimpse of the stars.

The Doghouse Tavern is everything his aunt promised—right on the shore overlooking a sun-swept, and yet sometimes shadowy view of the water. After handily putting away our hot dogs, salmon, vegetable soup, and barbecued pork, I buy cookies for all as we leave the place.

As we walk out the door to the downtown area, we see the camera crew with all its gear and camera persons in an old pickup. We opt to watch the filming of the movie for a few minutes before returning the boys to their aunt's house.

The Langley downtown, already rather old-fashioned looking with its antique stores lining the street, has an old movie theater called the Clyde, which seems to be a focal point of the shooting. We watch as the camera rolls for the period piece, which seems to be set in the early 1900s.

"Action," the director calls.

As the pickup putters down main street, we see the extras who appear to be from a circus—oddities that one might expect to see under a big tent advertising Ripley's Most

Unbelievable Sights of All Times. There are twin girls with pigtails who are playing Siamese twins (we are sure that the computers will be able to reduce the four legs on the girls and show them as two on the screen), there are several midgets, and one giant of a policeman. The scene seems almost surreal, and I feel as if I am in one of Flannery O'Connor's pieces like *Wise Blood* or Carson McCuller's *The Heart Is a Lonely Hunter* watching all of the sideshow oddities of life. Since I have my video camera, I begin to film the makers of the film for a little while.

As I do, I begin to think about the videos I am currently making at John Brown University for assessment purposes. Every year at graduation time, I sit the English majors down and ask them a few questions about our program. I'm usually depressed by their answers, but then I know I tend to obsess about my teaching too much anyway. For instance, in the spring the students essentially said they didn't like multiple interpretations of poetry and would prefer the professor telling the class one interpretation based on her training and experience. I felt this was typical of the students' reactions in general— always wanting to be spoon-fed the material without having to work for meaning themselves—even the honors students.

When I asked for the strengths of the program, I heard from them that they liked my cinnamon rolls, but they said nothing about the academic content of my courses. I think I work on teaching—my preparation, my enthusiasm, my keeping up with current theory—and I guess I'd just like to hear something positive some year. I'm sure these thoughts reflect my insecurities, since deep in my heart—even though I graduated with honors from the University of Mississippi and was in Phi Kappa Phi and completed my masters and doctoral program with the same high grades—I've never felt as though I were smart enough somehow to teach in college, much less to chair an English department.

The honors students intimidate me with their brilliance. "They are the makers of the future," I think—just like these film stars. I have wished many times though that I could add something to their lives academically.

"I guess we'd better get back," Josh interrupts my daydreaming to say. "We have other company coming to my aunt's for supper tonight."

My reverie is broken, and I put the video camera over my shoulder to leave. We're all a bit disappointed I think not to have seen at least one of the main stars of the film.

As we pull the car up to the house in Clinton, we are met in the drive by the aunt and her sister. I say good-bye and good luck to the boys, and the aunt who owns the house pauses to talk to just me.

"Thank you," she says, "for taking my nephews to lunch today. I don't know of many college professors who would do that today. I do some writing on the importance of mentors in young people's lives, and I wanted you to know what an important role you have played in Josh's and Matt's lives."

I've never quite known what to say when someone gives me a compliment (again, my insecurities, I guess), but I murmur a "thank you," and we speed away again to catch the ferry back to Port Townsend.

I think, though, on the way back about what she's said to me, and I thank God for the encouragement He's given me. Perhaps she's right. There always have to be people behind the scenes (like the script girl, the gaffers, the cameramen). Not all of us can be the stars, but our roles are nonetheless crucial to the outcome of the film—or the story of one's life. "Do students really remember the person longer than they remember the lesson?" I wonder. I think of I Corinthians 14:1, which says in the Revised Standard Version, "Make love your aim and earnestly seek the spiritual gifts especially that you may prophesy." Could being a mentor, rather than a star teacher, actually be the more important quality?

Chapter Thirteen
Family Resemblances

The evening is damp and cool. There's a touch of fall in the moist air that surrounds us, and some yellowish-looking leaves are already falling to the ground as we make our way around the sidewalk. Garlan and I are taking a walk around the large, open area of Fort Worden in Port Townsend. The old, white military barracks line one side of the street, and the officers' houses face them on the opposite side as if in continual confrontation with the other. I can identify with the feeling. While I'm not quite playing the drill instructor Foley in *An Officer and a Gentleman* yelling at officer candidate Zack Mayo, I feel as though I might be. I hear "hup, two, three" in my head. I've taken my job seriously in the past few years of trying to whip both of us into—if not exactly in shape—people who get at least nine miles or so in per week of walking.

We've both watched the health news which purports and promises that even moderate exercise can extend our years and make them healthier. Yet every time we walk, I listen to a litany of complaints from my husband, "It's too cold; it's too hot; I'm getting shin splints; my feet are sore from the rocks; it's going to rain; I need to go to the bathroom" and on and on. Most of the time, however, we are successful in walking our two and one half or three mile route. I wonder if—when he is eighty and I am seventy-five—he'll turn to me as we sit together on the sofa and thank me for adding years to his life because of my nagging.

"HON, HON," he'll shout in my ear, "I SURE AM GLAD YOU MADE US WALK SO MUCH WHEN WE WERE YOUNGER." If that happens, I guess I'll smile then to myself and know I've been vindicated. I wonder if other wives have this much trouble motivating their husbands (as well as themselves) to be faithful to just moderate exercise.

On this particular evening, we speak of renting *An Officer and a Gentleman* once again in spite of the fact that we've seen it at the movies and numerous times on the television networks, interspersed with seemingly zillions of commercial breaks. We've just discovered, though, that Fort Worden was the scene of the movie, and we want to spot not only the location where we're currently walking but also other sights in the town. We think about the motel where Paula and Zack made love, and the bar, outside of which Zack gets to show off his martial arts skills.

As we near the end of the officers' housing row, we notice a large family gathered together obviously for a family reunion there (which is evidently quite a popular choice of location). They are in the process of posing on the front steps of one of the houses. When they see us coming, they seemingly all have the same idea at once, and they begin screaming, "You've come along at the perfect time. Would you take our pictures? That way we can all be in the photograph!"

As we step before the house, they all rush out with their

Vancouver B.C.

respective cameras and lay them at our feet like an offering. We are instructed to take two shots with each—pick them up one at a time, take the two pictures, and lay them down to the right. Each camera has its special instructions which are hollered to us by the owners at the appropriate time. We hope we get good shots for them.

As we complete our duty, we're invited to come in and have supper with them (someone is from Texas). They're having fresh salmon, and if not supper, they say, what about at least having dessert? We decline since we've already eaten and are trying to complete another full lap, eight-tenths of a mile more, before the free classical concert at the Joseph Wheeler Theater.

As we walk past the house and the family goes inside for their salmon supper, I think about the film Kimberly has been recommending for us to rent this summer. It's a French film called *Family Resemblances*. She's said we would like it. I begin to think about the family we've just taken umpteen pictures of and wonder, what their lives are really like underneath the smiles of all—which will be the visible reminders of their trip together at Fort Worden. I remember the opening lines of Tolstoy's *Anna Karenina*, "All happy families are alike but an unhappy family is unhappy after its own fashion."

I wonder what their family secrets are: Is there a father like Zach's in *An Officer and a Gentleman,* who thinks children are simply a deterrent to a happy lifestyle? Who has the motivation to bring a dream to completion like Zach because, as he says in the movie, "I got nowhere else to go"? Are there truly women like Paula and her friend, who live only to marry an officer in order to see the world with their husbands? Who takes personal responsibility so deeply that he would commit suicide if he fails like the David Keith character?

We each know our own story and its truths (or myths) that we've created. I remember a conversation with Kimberly in the car when we were returning home from church. She was eight, and Chris was four. "Do you submit to Daddy like the preacher was saying in church today, Mama?" she asked. The text had been from Ephesians, chapter five. Southern Baptists at their convention even passed a resolution that said, "Wives are to graciously submit to their husbands."

At that time, I said, "Of course, Kimberly, your daddy is the boss in our family."

Both she and Chris then went into a fit of giggles, which lasted all the way home to our house in Tontitown. I guess even then they knew illusion and reality often diverge.

On this night, I coax and whine to Garlan, "Just one more round, please!"

"No, it's cold and rainy. I'm going into the theater and get us a good seat," he says as he heads off in another direction.

Cold and tired of the battle between officer and gentleman, I surrender...but for this night only.

Chapter Fourteen
Makah Maidens

"Row, row, row—squabs—as fast as you can!" I can almost hear the commands of Captain Ahab as he pursues the great white whale. Today I stand before the exhibits in the Makah Museum in Neah Bay, Washington, and I, too, get caught up in the pursuit of the whale. It's as if I am Queequeg, and along with Ishmael and others, am in the eight-man canoe feeling the ocean spray across my face and the adrenaline in my body rising as high as the swells around us. "Today will be the day; today will be the day," I think to myself, that we discover the nature of good and evil in the universe about us. I read on the museum board about the pursuit of the whale and about the special lance that has been created especially for this day as life and death struggle together for primacy. I understand that once the fatal blow has been struck, one of us in the canoe must dive into the water and sew the whale's mouth shut so that his body will not sink into the water but float easily into shore. I hope that will be me. I understand the Native American way of utilizing well all that Nature gives and wasting nothing. "I am Lisa, the whale hunter," I dream for a moment.

"Do you want to walk the Cape Flattery trail?" Garlan asks me, and my daydreaming is once again broken.

"Sure," I say, "if we can find exactly where it is."

We both study the map located in the front of the facility

but are still confused by the directions. We ask the front desk person to tell us verbally. Since the trail was completed a couple of years ago (it overlooks the Pacific Ocean and is, I suppose, one of most northwest points of the continental United States), many visitors have come to the Makah Reservation to walk it. The trail winds around the base of a mountain and follows a gravel road for five miles. There are no signs for us uninitiated folks (I assume the Native Americans go there, as always, by instinct).

We've just had lunch at the only café in Neah Bay, which is the Makah Maiden. Instead of Indian fry bread and corn dishes, we find a menu of fish and chips, burgers, and meat loaf lunches. We notice a twelve-year-old Makah boy working there in the family business. His job is to give the customers menus, bus tables, and deliver drinks. I ask him before we leave how he likes working there. He replies with few words, "It's fun; I like it."

I liked it also when I was growing up—at least for the one month when Mama leased the only café in Tutwiler. It was the summer of 1957, and Pop had been dead for a couple of months. Mama decided she would run a restaurant on her own, and we got an opportunity to be entrepreneurs. Mam would work in the kitchen, along with a Negro woman, as a cook; Judy and I would help waitress tables; and Mama would be the head waitress as well as business manager.

Mississippi was having its usual hot, humid summer. The

afternoons would be long inside the café as we waited for the supper crowd to come in. Sometimes my monotony would be broken when the door would open and Alan Everett (a boy I had a crush on) would walk in and order a malt. Mama had given me special instructions (I guess a holdover from her old soda jerk days herself) to put just two scoops of ice cream in the silver container and to fill it to a certain level with milk, and chocolate malt. Knowing how much I liked thick shakes myself (and wanting to make an impression on Alan), I ignored her and filled the container almost to the rim with ice cream alone. I knew I'd have to pay a price if she discovered it (at least with the usual tongue lashing), but I'm not sure she ever knew. She'd be working on the books at a corner table and drinking coffee.

I loved getting tips for my waitressing. Mama didn't pay Judy and me any salary (this was long before the days of child labor laws for twelve year olds), but she said we could keep our tips. On the first Sunday we ran the café, Judy and I had gone to church. Mama had told us to come from church as fast as possible since she knew we'd be busy. When we got there, Mama was frantic and the café full of people wanting food. We did the best we could as the novices we were. As I put my tip money in my pockets, I was already anticipating what I could buy; I even succumbed to the temptation to pocket Judy's tips as well as mine which I knew was wrong but, nevertheless, irresistible. After the rush was over, Judy was complaining about not making much money compared to my tips. Mama knew immediately what had happened.

"Martha Elise, you took Judy's tips from her tables, didn't you?"

I had to be quick to think of an excuse. I knew the tongue-lashing was unavoidable this time.

"I just put them in my right-hand pocket because we were so busy," I lied, "until I could give them to her later. I put mine in my left-hand pocket."

I guess maybe Mama was so tired from the Sunday rush and the stress she simply accepted my tale, though I'm sure she knew the truth.

In just over a month, the experiment was over, and the café was returned to its rightful owners, who at least got a month's rest for themselves. Mama said the reason was that Mam got so tired and hot in the kitchen; I knew that was a fib just as much as my lying about Judy's tips. She couldn't handle the responsibility. She picked all of us up, and the four of us went to the Mississippi Gulf Coast for the rest of the summer—our experiment in running a café forever ended.

On this August day though, before Garlan and I leave the museum, I pay close attention to the role of the Makah women. Instead of getting to participate in the exciting whale adventures with the men, their jobs were three-fold: some got to hang about on the beach with their spears and kill seals, some got to make beautiful, intricately designed baskets like the picture and accompanying story of Helma Swan-Hunter Ward, and some of the grandmothers got to be hostesses in their long houses, feeding all the hungry mouths day in and day out.

Today, I'm happy that women have more choices about their lives. If we want to go whale hunting (as the Makahs recently did), we can. We don't have to waitress only or serve everyone else in the kitchen. We don't have to be confined to the shoreline. We can put on our hiking boots and feel the exhilaration of the Spanish explorer Pizarro as he overlooked the Pacific Ocean for the first time. We are conquerors.

Chapter Fifteen
The Gimmick

It's a cool August night in downtown Seattle as Kimberly, Sheri, and I walk briskly up the hills from Third and Pike Streets toward A Contemporary Theater on Seventh Street. Tonight it will be featuring a one-woman play called *The Gimmick,* which was written by Dael Orlandersmith, an African-American performer. As we settle into our seats, we step across the set for the play, which is simply a cushiony white background with its accompanying flooring. It has given the three of us the sensation of walking through a cloud.

As the performance begins, Orlandersmith speaks of the character's life, Alexis, in Harlem and her long friendship and problematic relationship with a friend whose name was Jimmy. Periodically, the signifiers—red, purple, and black—flash up on the screen along with the signified shades that are represented. She moves us from their meeting and immediate bonding through their changing moods in adolescence and ultimately to the final breech that occurs in their friendship.

She speaks of artists in general and poses the question that many ask, "How can two people from similar backgrounds and environments turn out so differently?" In the characters' lives, Alexis confronts her demons but overcomes them with the help of a mentor librarian, Miss Innes, while Jimmy sinks into a life of drugs and ultimately dies of an overdose. Alexis becomes a writer, and Jimmy's artistic talent dies with him.

It's like a déjà vu experience for me as I lose my concentration on the play at times and think about my friendship with Prentiss. We were in the same classes at West Talla-hatchie when I began eighth grade there after Pop died. I noticed his gentleness probably before I noticed his handsome looks. He was well mannered and quiet, and I, on the other hand, was gregarious and determined to get his attention. We often were sitting close to one another in class, and I'd do silly things like drop my pencil in front of his desk to see if he would pick it up for me. He always did, and I had an opportunity to gaze longingly into his eyes. The first time it happened, I was the one who was surprised since I noticed that one of his eyes was green and the other blue—I'm sure a genetic characteristic for many others, but I had never seen it before.

By the time we got to the tenth grade, we had spoken some together, but not a lot. I knew he was shy but that eventually I'd win him over. That year we were in Coach Cox's class for world history. Most of the time Coach spent his time in two ways: one, standing by his office at the end of the hall popping students with a rolled-up towel, or two, sitting on his desk telling war stories, trying to gross the girls out, we thought, with his tales of mustard gas in World War I and soldiers coughing up their lungs as they died. He also gave instructions to the boys in class about how to treat girls on dates—to be gentlemen always and open the car door for their dates. When test time came around at the end of each chapter or so, he'd simply tell us to read the book and prepare. He'd give us one of the tests that accompanied the textbook.

Since the class time was of so little value, I would often take out my compact, lipstick, and mirror and pretend to redo my makeup. Prentiss usually sat behind me, and I would sneak a peak at him in the mirror. After a couple of times, he caught on and would wink at me. I knew I was finally making progress in my pursuit of him.

In the fall, the other kids seemed to realize we were attracted to one another even before Prentiss knew it and voted us sophomore class favorites. By spring we were boyfriend and girlfriend—going steady. I got to wear his letter jacket—and did—even on the warmest Mississippi days. One afternoon we had both stayed after school for a track meet and were standing outside the gym. He leaned over and kissed me. At age fifteen it was my first real kiss, and I loved his tenderness and the love I felt for him at that moment.

It wasn't long though before we both went on to another girlfriend (Linda for him, the girl he would later marry) and another boyfriend (John E. for me), but I think the power of a first love is strong. When we met again at our tenth-year class reunion in 1972, his hair had begun to turn prematurely gray. I was seven and one-half months pregnant with Chris and had Kimberly with me as a three year old. We talked and probably both wondered what might have been between us had our choices been different.

Shortly after that I heard from my friend Beverly that Prentiss had separated from his wife. Later he died in a small plane crash while smuggling drugs. By that time, I had completed a bachelor's and a master's degree and had taught in college for one year. I too reflect on Orlandersmith's question and seek an answer: In similar environments, which easily promote failure, why does one go forward while another does not? Like Hamlet, my interrogatives far outweigh the answers.

Chapter Sixteen
Inward Renewals

Our time here in limbo is ending since we'll be moving on to our final destination of the odyssey in a another week or so. Cindy has sent our rental agreement for our cabin in Skagway, and we have dutifully forwarded the $400 deposit to her. It's located two miles outside of Skagway on Dyea Road and has a rather interesting history. According to Cindy, it was originally a float house in Pelican, which she put on the river and floated to Skagway. Since the house arrived, she has added to it so that now it has several rooms and one and one-half baths.

An imperceptible change has occurred within my inner being over the last three months in northwest Washington, and I'm not sure when and where it took place—I've lost my cynicism.

I know that for two reasons. I noticed it one night this week as I was reading Judy Blume's adult novel, *Summer Sisters,* which I picked up on the sale table at the Jefferson County Library—fifty cents isn't a bad deal for a 1998 piece. It was late when I read about the main character's cynicism (maybe the author's as well). Vix, the protagonist, is from a family of four children; the youngest of the kids (Nathan) has muscular dystrophy. As she thinks about his life and the very real possibility that he won't live much longer, she goes through her family's clichés—of God's giving them a special gift since He knew they would provide a lot of love for him. She then poses the clinker of a question, "What gift did God give Nathan?"

I have to admit that in the past I would have also parroted the question to myself cynically, "Yeah, what GIFT did God give Nathan?" But now I find myself pondering Judy Blume's question more deeply. I conclude that God gave him life, he also gave him the possibility of salvation and spending eternity with Him in a perfect body, and He gave him a family who loved him deeply. All in all, that ain't bad.

The other reason I know my cynicism is evaporating is that yesterday I was combing my hair and seeing all the gray. I was thinking that I look so much like Mama, now that I'm aging. For the thirty years before she died, her hair was gray. I've always covered mine with color since we all seem to resist somehow the idea of turning into our mothers. Since I've been reading her journals, letters to Kimberly, and travelogue to Skagway this summer, I've become incredibly closer to her in spirit. As I looked into the mirror, instead of my usual cynical attitude about aging, I simply thought, "Well, that's okay. I really don't mind looking like Mother. She was quite a gal."

I started thinking about how change takes place within each one of us when we're on an active search for meaning. According to *Webster's Third New International Dictionary,* the word *odyssey* has a couple of meanings: 1. a long wandering: a series of adventurous journeys usu. marked by many changes of fortune, and 2. an extensive intellectual or spiritual wandering or quest. I think my odyssey encompasses both definitions.

This morning I was reading from 2 Corinthians 4 and was reminded of the truth of verse 16, where the apostle Paul was giving instructions to the early Christians, "Therefore we do not lose heart. Even though our outward man is perishing, yet the inward man is being renewed day by day." I know that one way we move forward spiritually is by listening to what God is teaching us through His Word.

I think though that there are also a number of other ways in which we grow. We learn from the lessons of nature if we're attentive to its voice. Even scientists revere the intricacy of a rainbow or the inner workings of a wildflower.

We learn through other cultures. Yesterday Garlan and I were listening to Elaine at the final outdoor performance of the summer in Port Townsend. She is of the Jamestown-Clallam Native American tribe. She reminded us once again that we should be respectful to our ancestors, to listen to their voices and their wisdom. She told of the myth of the coyote fur in the trees (all because a coyote envied the bear and the eagle and wanted to be like them instead of who he was) and of Slapoo, the witch-like woman who would take children away with her to the woods if they misbehaved. We all use the oral tradition to teach our children and to warn them of good and evil in the world.

We learn through the visual, aural, and performing arts.

An example from film recently is Spielberg's *Amistad,*which shows an African slave who comes to God by viewing the beautifully illustrated photographs of Jesus in the Bible. Tolstoy said, "Art is not a handicraft; it's a feeling . . ."

We learn through our mentors—those people who saw a glimpse of hope within us at some point in our lives and chose to invest their time and energy in teaching us. I think of Mrs. Berry, my junior high English teacher, who worked so hard as a teacher to help us rural kids go beyond the poetic line to the period rather than read in sing-song voices and pause at the end of each line. I still share her excitement for stories like O'Henry's "The Gift of the Magi," which she played on the record player for us on the day we got out for Christmas vacation, or for Dickens' *David Copperfield,* which showed us there's hope for even the poorest of the poor—like his main character and like most of us at West Tallahatchie.

And last, but perhaps one of the most important, we learn from attaching meaning to our memories. As this time in Washington comes to a close, I believe that I will learn more, but instead of a small, inner voice I think I will hear more of other people's stories as they cope with life in one of the most beautiful, but one of the most remote and coldest, states in the United States.

Chapter Seventeen
A Fitting Finale

Today we prepare for a one-week trip back to Little Rock, where our ten-month-old granddaughter, Caitlyn, and her parents live. After we return, we'll head up to our destination of Skagway. I'm excited about both trips, but I know there's at least one item of unfinished business to do before I leave the Port Hadlock, Washington, house.

I go back into Kathy's office, pick up the Seattle telephone book and turn to the section entitled "Charities." Several months ago Doris, Nelson's sister, and I talked about the love seat that belonged to Mama and Nelson. At Judson Park, his retirement center, he had it in his room close by his bed. Now, however, that he's being moved to Stage Three of the center, the most severely disabled section, he no longer has room for it. Without thinking, I quickly volunteered to take the love seat back home with me to Siloam Springs in Arkansas. As usual, my impulsive action has gotten me into trouble.

I can't help it though; we are always sentimental about our furniture. In our home in Arkansas, we have the bedroom suite that belonged to Mam and Pop in the 1950s in their little white house in Tutwiler, and in another bedroom, we have the first bedroom set we bought for Kimberly as a two year old. We're that way about cars as well. When we sold our 1990 Oldsmobile Ciera, which we bought to celebrate our twenty-fifth

anniversary, and our 1991 Geo Tracker in order to have money
for our trip to Alaska, we almost cried. I know other people
must have similar feelings. I often wonder if there's a support
group for people who simply can't get rid of their stuff long
after their usefulness or beauty has fled.

I've actually never seen another love seat like this particular one. Mama and Nelson bought it about the time they moved
to Huntsville, Alabama, three years after their marriage. It is a
rocker in basic chocolate brown with multi-colored squares of
earth colors across the back. It represents home. In Alabama,
Nelson was working for Boeing Aircraft Company during the
time when the space program was at its zenith. They rented a
house called Seven Pines by its owners.

Kimberly was Caitlyn's age when we started making the
frequent weekend trips to Huntsville. We were tired students
and parents then at the University of Mississippi, and the
prospect of a relaxing fall or winter weekend beckoned us like
Calypso to Odysseus to come and stay awhile.

Even though it was the late 1960s, we felt strangely divorced by
the upheavals going on throughout the world—the assassinations of the
Kennedys and Martin Luther King, the racial unrest between the Ku
Klux Klan and the Jewish community in south Mississippi, the murders
of Sharon Tate and friends in Hollywood, and the protests at Kent State
with the deaths of the students. We were simply focused on baby,
study, and professional careers, which we hoped lay ahead for us.
We were never tempted by the attractions of the lotus flowers

(hashish) though we knew others were.

At Mama's we never had to fight for the love seat; we knew Mama and Nelson would relinquish it to us for a weekend at least. We would sit with Kimberly, who wasn't quite walking yet, standing between us, looking over the back, waving her toys around. When she'd get tired, we'd rock her to sleep in front of the fireplace, which was crackling with its dry-wooded mix of oak and pine. When she got fussy, Nelson would sprinkle a magical mixture of multi-colored chemicals into the fire, which would then burn blue, red, and orange for her entertainment, and ours as well.

When Mama and Nelson moved to Seattle in the early 1970s, they didn't consider doing anything else but taking the love seat with them. As I would visit them there through the years, I would often see them sit in it together holding hands as they relived memories of Mama's life as a single mom, Nelson's wartime experiences as a twenty-one-year-old volunteer in the Air Force, and their concerns about their children and their growing families. When Mama was diagnosed with chronic lymphatic leukemia in the fall of 1980, it then became easier for her to lie most of the day on the regular-length sofa instead.

After I volunteered to take the love seat back home with me and got on the phone to see how it could be done, reality set in. I discovered there was simply no way to do it easily. We had first thought about renting a small trailer, but Kimberly talked us out of that decision, saying she would be very concerned about our safety through all the traffic in southern

California. We called several of the big moving companies and discovered they required 2,700 pounds before they would give us a section of the truck. We checked with the largest freight company in the nation, who required that the love seat be totally ready for pickup by crating it properly. Even then the cost was prohibitive as two movers would be required.

I tried repeatedly to develop some type of a wooden horse plan like Odysseus, but I had to surrender finally. That's why I search now for a charity to donate the love seat to. My first idea is to try the Salvation Army as I knew they had trucks and would sometimes pick up donations. For some reason, their number wasn't listed under the "Charities" section. I peruse the page for other ads that promise a pickup. I first contact a charity for the blind.

"Hello, I was wondering if you would pick up a piece of furniture I have to donate to your charity?" I inquire.

"No, sorry, we don't take furniture, but I can give you the name of a charity that will."

She then gives me the number of the local Union Gospel Rescue Mission. Again I explain my dilemma to Bob, the volunteer who answers the phone. At first he is reluctant to accept the love seat either since it's currently stored in a locker in Des Moines.

"We haven't had the best of luck meeting people at storage lockers," he hedges.

I'm discouraged, but it is at this time that I suddenly remember that Daddy stayed frequently at the Union Gospel Rescue Missions (there are some 250 of them across the United States) whenever he was broke and down on his luck again. He knew he could get a free, warm bed, eat a good, hot meal, listen to an evangelical sermon, and be on his way to catch a new boat the next morning.

"You know, Bob, I've just remembered that my father, who was an alcoholic, used to stay in your mission a lot when he was alive. I know my Mama would be pleased to know that the furniture went to your charity."

I don't know if Bob is just tired of my persistence, or if what I've said hits a responsive chord, but he relents. "O.K." he says, "we'll do it."

As I hang up the phone after the arrangements are made, I begin to marvel at God's sense of humor. I've just been reading Phillip Roth's novel once again, *Goodbye Columbus,* in preparation for teaching a class in Modern Jewish Literature next spring, in which he refers to an old Hebrew proverb. We humans make plans for this and that and tell God what we are going to do, but according to Roth, the prophetic words, "God only laughs," sum up our incredible pomposity. We are wee humans and can never compare our plans to the greatness of His.

Chapter Eighteen
The Caitlyn Interlude

One of the definitions of the word *interlude* is that it is entertainment between acts of a play. I like that definition, I think to myself, as I carry my ten month old granddaughter, Caitlyn, across the street from her house to a neighborhood park. We've been back in Little Rock for less than twenty-four hours, and I've found I've fallen madly in love with my granddaughter once again. At this halfway point of my sabbatical, just before we head north to Alaska for the fall, I can't think of being anywhere better for the next week. Even though it's been just three months since we've been away, I know that a baby's heart forgets easily the relationship we had established earlier. Nevertheless, this particular baby shows no sign of strangeness in warming up to us again. She doesn't cling to her parents but willingly stretches out her arms to us.

In the morning, we put her in her stroller and decided to take a power walk up and down the hills of the city. What we had forgotten so easily, however, is that we're back in the deep South with all of its accompanying heat and humidity. The forecast is for the mid 90s, and sweat begins to drip from our faces and soak our clothes a mere two blocks from the house. Early September shows no sign of cooler fall weather.

In the park this afternoon, just the two of us explore the options for both learning and bonding. One of Kimberly's early memories of when we moved to Springdale is going to the library and feeding the ducks in our neighborhood park. She was three then and didn't know until she was practically grown that we had the same activity every day because we were too poor to do anything else. Garlan was just beginning his job at Springdale Memorial Hospital, and I was a stay-at-home mom expecting our second child.

I hope this park visit together with Caitlyn will be the first of many in the years ahead. We go to the tire-like swing in the middle of the park, and I place her on it. With one hand, she holds the chain link support on the right, and I hold her hand at the left. She doesn't show any emotion but seems to enjoy the gentle breeze blowing through her dark hair. Next we try the slide; I place her about half way up the kid-size equipment and take her slowly down. She's not quite as accepting of this as she was the swing, so we meander over to the trees to have a look at the leaves. I tell her, "Caitlyn, God made the leaves on the tree. God made the trees. God made Caitlyn and loves her very much." She smiles because I am smiling.

A car drives up in the distance, and three young Asian boys come bounding into the park. Their mothers follow shortly after. Caitlyn is fascinated by this intrusion on our time together and follows their activities closely as they play on the jungle gym with its many bright colors as it winds willy nilly this way and that.

We watch the boys play for a long while; Caitlyn shows no sign of impatience. We begin to walk toward her house, and without thinking, I sit down on the merry-go-round with her on my lap and begin to croon in my old, out-of-tune voice, "Hush, little baby, don't say a word. Mama's gonna buy you a mockingbird..."

I begin to think of Chris, my son and now Caitlyn's daddy. I marvel at the outstanding man he has become—a professional in his career but also a loving father to his baby girl. I also begin to think about Caitlyn's future as a millennial baby as well as past traditions for women in the world. I'd like to think that her world (as well as the Asian boys' world) will be free of discrimination. The feminist movement of the 1970s has brought about great gains for us as women. The racial unrest of the 1960s has brought about more acceptance for all regardless of race or color (a true miracle in the South). The one area where much controversy still exists is that of sexual orientation. Just recently Kimberly said she was glad that some couples were choosing to raise their children without reinforcing sexual stereotypes. She reported the following conversation between two young girls and their Mama:

"Mama, I'm going to marry Katie when we get older."

The parent's response did not revert to the traditional dialogue of the past. "Now, honey, you know you're a girl. Girls don't marry girls, but they must marry boys." Instead, the response was "Sure, if you want to marry Katie when you're older, that would be fine."

I wish I could see into Caitlyn's world by 2025 (and maybe

I'll be able to with the advances in modern medicine and longevity since I'll be a mere eighty). As I envision her future, I want to see her most of all:

A young woman who loves God and loves and cares for her neighbors, whether they be next door or across the world;

A woman who can have a career or lifestyle of her choice without judgment by society, or the church, for her decision;

A woman who can live in a world that will be safer for her—that as a society we will be able to make vast improvements in the social problems that continue to plague us: sexual and physical abuse of children and women, alcoholism, and divorce;

A woman who will stay as relaxed as she is right now as a baby and will enjoy nature as a source of inspiration and an evidence of God's creative powers;

A woman who will develop her aesthetic appreciation of art, music, literature, films, and theater;

A woman who values the importance of learning every day for the rest of her life;

A woman who will respect her heritage from both the Whiteside and the Brandom sides: Mam and Pop, who loved one another deeply and sacrificed greatly for our country; her great-grandmothers, Frances and Anna Belle, who were brave in spite of many years of pain; her Mama B and Papa B (Garlan and I) who will never be able to love her enough; and her Aunt Kimberly, who is everything a woman is.

And lastly, A woman who is not afraid to be an activist in the causes she deems important.

Chapter Nineteen
The Mystery of Eyebrows

Eyebrows have been a source of mystery in our family for many years, since they keep appearing and disappearing. I guess the outside world also shares in this fascination too since we've all been intrigued through the years by Groucho Marx's set of eyebrows, which he used effectively for comedic purposes. We can close our eyes now and see him raise his eyebrows repeatedly back from behind those horn-rimmed glasses, and we laugh at our memories. When Fonzie was introduced as a character on Happy Days on the 1970s TV show, both Kimberly and Chris were endlessly talking of how his eyebrows went across the top of his eyes without a break. Finally, I guess, even the cool Fonz got the word and had them plucked into a reasonable appearance.

Today Garlan and I have come to the Judson Park Health Center to say good-bye to Nelson for three months since we're finally on our way north to Alaska for the fall. He appears particularly frail today as he battles advanced Parkinson's disease. It seems to be the victor and he the loser. It may be the medication, which is to render his shaking limbs still, but as his supper tray is delivered into the room, he struggles to make his seemingly paralyzed hand bend in order to feed himself. His sister Doris and her husband, Dick, are also there. We've just come from the airport from our trip to Little Rock and our visit with our angel, Caitlyn.

The four of us make small talk—anything to keep the
focus away from Nelson's painful attempts in remaining somewhat self-sufficient by feeding himself. Doris has promised to
give me Pop's Bible which Mama had given to another sister in
Nelson's family. It is wrapped in bubble wrap; I'm tempted to
look at it now, but out of politeness, I defer my goal until we return to Kimberly and Sheri's apartment on Queen Anne Hill.

I glance at Nelson and, once again, am quite surprised that
he has no eyebrows. This phenomenon wouldn't be so remark-
able except for the fact that for years he painted on himself huge,
black eyebrows. It was always a family mystery from the first
time we met him back in the early '60s. We understood why
women would paint eyebrows on themselves but why a man?

The subject even became the focus of some hilarious moments within the family. On one particular occasion in 1989,
Mama and Nelson had come to Arkansas for a visit. We did our
usual celebration dinner before they left, and all sat around a large
table at Red Lobster. Mama had ordered her favorite—stuffed
shrimp—and all was going well until the big question. It came
from Kimberly's first serious boyfriend, Brian, who was sitting
down at the other end of the table.

"I was wondering about your eyebrows, sir. Were you in
an accident, a fire or something?"

The table went immediately silent because all of us knew
this was a taboo topic (it's a Southern thing to speculate endlessly about various and sundry situations but always behind

the back of the star of the gossip). We sat for what seemed like an endless time waiting for some type of response. Nelson sat absolutely silent and never responded. At last, I remarked on the delicious nature of the salads before us, and we all went on to other topics.

Maybe I felt the need to bring the situation back to normalcy since perhaps I, of all the others at the table, might have the key to the mystery of the eyebrows. I had created a mystery as well in the family when I was about eight or nine years old when my own eyebrows disappeared.

I can hear Mama with her shrill voice quizzing me now. "Martha Elise, what has happened to your eyebrows?"

"I don't know," I lied, and shuffled from one foot to another, as usual, in uncomfortable situations that I didn't want to confront either.

In reality I had always had a problem with hair pulling. First, I was around five and would pull great hunks of hair from my head, that is, until I was with Mama at the beautician's one day (long before the word *hair stylist* came into fashion) and showed the woman fixing Mama's hair one of my hair trophies.

"I just pulled out this hunk of hair," I announced proudly.

"Honey," she said as she looked into my face so seriously, "don't ever pull out your hair. That's an awful thing to do."

I guess I didn't think about eyebrows also being hair because I then went to them as a source for plucking. One by one over the next few years, they all disappeared.

I now know that this behavior, along with nail biting (which I still do occasionally), foot swinging and other fidgety behaviors, and laughing in inappropriate situations can all be signs of anxiety. I'm much more relaxed now that I know more about psychology and have eliminated practically all such behaviors until I get into a situation that I feel is out of my control. Then they return quickly as if I'm five years old again.

I suspect the same was true for Nelson. He was a mere twenty-year-old when he volunteered for the Air Force in 1942 in War World II. After receiving a few short months of training, he was flying up to eight reconnaissance or bombing missions over the enemy. It is difficult to imagine the stress that he, as well as all our military serving in any war, must have been experiencing. Not knowing when one climbed into the plane whether there would be a natural end to the day—and yet knowing that there had been no time for cross-training by the military so that, if the navigator took a hit, the plane would likely not get back to its destination—would have been harrowing circumstances for the best of us. In any event, I think I solved the mystery of Nelson's painted eyebrows.

As we bend to say good-bye to Nelson this day, he takes our leaving very hard. Great tears begin to fall from his eyebrowless eyes. I hope we'll meet again in December when we are coming home from the Skagway adventure. If not, then I am convinced we'll see each other in eternity. I thank him, in my heart, for the years of care that he gave Mama through her emotional and physical illnesses. I wish that all stepfathers today were as honorable as both Nelson and Pop; I salute them both.

Part Three:

The Destination

Chapter Twenty
Jonah, Whales, and Lisa

It's the morning of September 13, and we've arisen early in order to catch our ferry here at Port Hardy on its route to Prince Rupert—a fifteen-hour trip. We're supposed to be at the ferry dock at 6:30, but as usual, we're excited about our trip and have slept restlessly through the night, awaiting our departure. Our motel in this small, sleepy town in northern British Columbia has at least given us a bed, a meal in its restaurant downstairs, and a view of the water. Last evening late we saw from our window a bald eagle sitting on a post.

As we arrive early at the dock, we discover that everyone else has arrived at the same time. The morning is slightly foggy and eerie almost. We expect to see Poe's Raven, who is still sitting "evermore" on the bust of the goddess, Pallas Athena. Our attention immediately focuses on the ferry boat, which sits in the water staring at us looking like a monstrous whale that has opened its mouth for us to enter into.

We willingly submit to its power and drive inside when the ferry worker gives us the command, along with the others waiting for their journey inside. I think of Jonah and wonder if we have anything in common.

God had given Jonah a command to go to Ninevah and preach to the thousands of people there, urging them to repent and accept Him as the One and only true God. Yet he had

rebelled. Instead of going directly to his destination, which
was northeast, he went instead in the opposite direction, west
to Tarshish. As a result of that decision (thanks to free will
given to us by God at our creation), he was thrown from the
ship he was on while the sea was tempestuous, and then swal-
lowed immediately by a great whale, in whose belly he spent three
days and nights. Scholars argue over whether the episode is to be
taken literally or symbolically. Our Southern Baptist Church theology believes in the infallibility and literalness of all Scripture, so the
subject is closed (except for my individual conclusion, of course).

After singing hymns of praise to God (I'd certainly be doing
a lot of praising and praying myself in similar circumstances),
God whispered into the ear of the whale to spit Jonah out onto
dry land. This time Jonah had no problem with obedience. He
preached to the people of Nineveh, who wholeheartedly began to
repent and fast. God had mercy and spared their lives. If taken literally, one would have to wonder about the appearance of Jonah
after three days and nights in the belly of the whale. Perhaps that
was enough alone to scare the people into repentance.

But Jonah hadn't totally learned God's lesson. These people were enemies of Israel; Jonah wanted God to slay them all
in the forty days as He had promised. He decided to sulk by sitting under a gourd and watching to see what God would do. God
once again showed His sense of humor, as well as His incredible mercy; he had a worm (ever notice that the whales and
worms don't have any trouble with obedience) eat the leaves of

the gourd until Jonah was burning with heat and thirst and complaining that he'd rather be dead than hot (Mississippi days also make one think that way). God spared them all, but not without a final word to Jonah: Remember to focus on other people; do not be so self-absorbed with your own comfort.

It is somewhat ironic then that the New Testament shows Jesus comparing Himself to just one other person, Jonah. We look at those few verses in Matthew 12: 39–41 and don't immediately see the similarities. But Christ is quick to make the lesson plain; just as Jonah was in the whale's belly for three days and nights, so shall the Son of Man be. In other words, He would arise to life once again after being buried for three days.

Perhaps the lesson God taught to Jonah, however, has another similarity. Since Christ was the son of Mary, an earthly woman, he also had free will and the ability to decide on obedience or disobedience with God's plan. Although it must have been unbelievably difficult for Him (He sweat drops of blood in the garden), He chose to focus on other people rather than His own upcoming death on a cross.

As I'm thinking about Jonah, whales, and me, I notice that we have pulled away from the dock, albeit about thirty minutes later than scheduled. It's a beautiful sunny day, and we know the scenery will be spectacular as we wind through the Inside Passage on our journey. In a couple of hours, the purser announces that whales have been spotted portside. Practically all of the people in our section leap up with their videos and Nikons to cap-

ture the moment. As the day lingers into the evening hours, we
spot at least two other groups of whales spouting their water
above, seemingly unaware of the splashes they're creating with
the on-board crowd.

I guess I'm hoping that in some ways this trip will be my
whale-Ninevah experience as well. I think I've been so angry
at God for the past ten years that I've been like Jonah—pout-
ing under a leafless gourd. Why? Simply because my own little world hasn't always been perfect. I've discovered flaws in
myself finally (after a fight with a girlfriend a few years back,
she told me, "You think you're Miss Perfect!"). I think of all
the opportunities I've squandered in ministering to other people
because of my own selfish attitude and comfort. I know that
being in the belly of the whale for three months in Skagway (its
tiny population of 700 and isolation may be similar to Jonah's
experience) is bound to teach me more lessons about life. May
I open my eyes to see and my ears to hear.

Chapter Twenty-one
Independent Women

As I think about my own maternal lineage, as well as the legacy that I'll leave, I realize independent women have been haunting my family for at least four generations. I wonder if Caitlyn will also be one; I really can't see that she won't, however, since her Mama is very independent as well. I tend to think that we're not that alone or unusual, especially in northern British Columbia and Alaska.

After our ferry trip to Prince Rupert, we're on our way by car east to Highway 37, which is billed as the fastest way to Alaska. On the way, we see numerous little camps set up by rivers. They all announce a woman's name followed by the word Depot— Mary's Depot, Debbie's Depot, and so on. We think they might have something to do with the salmon fishing perhaps in the fall, but we're generally baffled. We hope the road will be good, and it is—until the turnoff to Stewart, where it then becomes a combination of pavement, loose gravel, and mud. After driving the first fifteen miles, we see road construction signs ahead, and a woman motions for us to park behind the road equipment.

"You just missed the lead car; you'll have eighteen minutes to wait for it to return. It's a five-mile stretch," she announces.

Tentatively, I poke my head out on the driver's side and hopefully inquire, "Does the road improve after this stretch?"

"Honey, it's just beginning; you have no idea," we're told.

"Since we've had so much rain last year it's been in awful condition."

She eats a sandwich as she holds her sign. I think it's a bit unusual to have lunch so late in the afternoon (3:30 p.m.) but think I might as well pass the time with a bit of conversation as we wait the eighteen minutes.

"Late lunch, I see," I venture.

"Yes, I ordered it this morning, but it's just been delivered."

I look around, knowing that we haven't seen any cafés or even gas stations for miles and miles.

"Where do you have to go to get it?" I inquire.

"Oh, it comes from Dease Lake." she says, "All of us live up there. It's about three and one-half hours north."

"Surely you don't commute every day?" I say incredulously.

"We've got cabins nearby where we stay," she replies. "I pay my workers $20 an hour, and jobs are scarce."

"My name is Lisa," I say. "We are on our way to Alaska for the fall."

"I'm Wendy," she replies. "I own this construction company, Wendy O's."

"How did you get to be the owner of a construction company?" I'm curious by this time for sure. Since the feminist movement, it's not unusual in the United States to see women construction workers, but this woman is the boss of her own company. I'm impressed.

"I'm a registered nurse, and I was on my way to New

Zealand last year, but family problems prevented me from going. My husband and I divorced, and I suddenly found myself a single mom of two boys. The oldest is about to graduate in a year. I took every cent I could get ahold of and put it into this business."

"It seems to be going well then, and you certainly have your job cut out for you. Oh, before we go," I say, "I wanted to ask you about the little depot signs we've seen every few miles on our trip through here. What are those exactly? Do they fish there or what?"

"Oh, those," she replies, "they're mushroom depots. Mushrooms sell for $60 a pound, and college students and others come up all the time to gather mushrooms. They can make $1,000 day sometime—of course, they're not likely to report it."

I wonder about Debbie and Mary who run the depots. I assume they serve as middle women, collecting the mushrooms and shipping them to buyers elsewhere, paying the students in cash for their day's labor—more ingenious independent women —but I worry about where the law stands on all this seemingly illegal activity. Since jobs are scarce for everyone, do they feel they have no choice but to take such a risk? Are they also single Mamas who must feed a hungry bunch of kids? I'd have to talk to one for some answers, I suppose.

About this time we see the lead car returning in the distance. We don't even bother to look at the map since Wendy would have to know the precise traveling time to Dease Lake. We had hoped to make it to the intersection of Highway 37 with the Alaskan Highway (No. 1) before we stopped overnight but now realize that goal was too hopeful with the poor road conditions.

We say good-bye to Wendy O. and continue our journey north. By morning, we are rested enough to begin the journey once more on Highway 37. I tell Garlan that I hope someone at the end of the highway will be selling t-shirts that say, "I traveled the length of Highway 37 and survived!" I start to imagine the many pioneer women of the last century who did this without the convenience of modern transportation.

Since it's the middle of September, we are absolutely stunned by the spectacular scenery about us. We don't even mind the slow drive at 35 mph as much since the black cottonwoods and aspens are in full color of golds and pale yellows contrasting to the deep green shades of the evergreens. The background is of snow-peaked mountains, and for a moment I feel as if I've been transported to a Van Gogh painting. While not a field of sunflowers, the colors around us are more vibrant than I ever imagined. I take out my video and Minolta to try to capture a bit of God's artwork.

We're both hungry by the time we get to our Alaskan Highway, and just as we had hoped, there's a café and service station open. The café is small with masculine decorations about— moose heads hanging on the walls with their huge antlers and other such decor. The clientele is all male. In the cafe is a lone woman who evidently runs the place completely by herself— she's waitress, cook, dishwasher, hostess, bookkeeper, and grocery purchaser.

I ask her how long she's been working there. She doesn't give an exact date but says she started in the cafe-business when she was practically a child since her Mama owned it. I gather she's grown up in the business there and wouldn't consider any other job. She's now middle-aged like us.

I'm impressed when she announces that the bread is homemade. I'm sure she bakes it every day for the customers' enjoyment—another time-consuming chore in her already busy workday. When breakfast arrives, I can tell that the customers must have appetites far bigger than mine. It's difficult for the plate to hold it all, but we manage to eat every bite anyway as if we are log workers and actually need to eat that many calories for the morning ahead. Instead, we tell her good-bye and wish her well, instinctively believing that she would be working there still if we ever returned.

As we drive on the Alaskan Highway, which our country's servicemen built during World War II, it's wonderful compared to Highway 37. We begin to relax more and get the speedometer up to the legal 100 kilometers. We are in the Yukon Territory. I remember that Pop was with Mam for about a month in the town of Whitehorse during the war. I'm anxious to explore the town, but we're so tired after traveling six days, we opt for a later trip and head south on the Klondike Highway (No. 2) to Skagway, our final destination.

Cindy, our landlady, is talking on the phone when we drive

up to her place just off Dyea Road in Skagway. We fall in love immediately with our home for the next three months. Cindy explains all of the quirky little aspects we need to know for two southern people to survive in such a harsh climate even in the fall—how to plug in the heat tapes when the temperature falls to around twenty degrees. She's on her way to Juneau by ferry to leave a car with her sister to be repaired over the winter. She's a dervish of activity; we are sure she's a native Alaskan.

"By the way you move around, Cindy," I say in order to get to know a bit of her story, "you must be a native."

"No, actually, I'm from southern California. I've been here a few years though. I bought the cabin about five years ago. Since then I've added on to the side and put the bedroom in upstairs. There are three guest cabins I rent in the tourist season."

Like the other women we've met on this trip, Cindy is also an independent woman. She's on her way, after the Juneau trip, to Fairbanks. She doesn't mind the thought at all of a thirteen-hour trip alone.

I'm the mother hen though and say, "You might have to spend the night on the way, huh?"

"No, it gets lighter and lighter the farther north you go," and she's off.

I know that these stories are likely just the beginning of many we'll hear in the next three months of both current and past independent women. After all, Skagway was the gateway for the famous Alaskan Gold Rush in 1898. Wherever there are men, there'll also be women—and I bet the ones who came out then were also very independent.

Chapter Twenty-two
The Connection

It's September 20, and today is the day that I've been wait-
ing for since I was a child. I think I'm eight years old again, and
I feel that euphoria that sometimes only a child can feel as
Garlan and I hear the whistle of the White Pass and Yukon train.
We're escorted as a group about a block down the line by one
of the railway employees.

"Please get on the first two cars. There's plenty of room,
so no one needs to push or shove. You will all get a good seat,"
she jokes.

Most of us in the crowd are middle aged and hopefully past
a lot of the pushing and shoving of youth now that we are in our
slower, more patient days. We represent the "locals," as they're
called here in Skagway. The other railway cars are completely full
since they are the cruise ship tourists who have booked the ride as
part of their enjoyment of their day in Skagway.

I look at the prices of the tickets and am glad for new-found
friends here in town. In talking with the director of tourism a few
days back, a local character by the name of Buckwheat, we were
offered two free passes. Like most of the people in Skagway, I
suspect Buckwheat is a true Alaskan man. It seems as if the
majority of folks here must dibble and dabble in a number of
small business ventures in order to make a decent living. For
example, the video store has a hodgepodge of wares within its

walls. Not only can one check out the latest releases (I'm already missing a theater here), but one can also buy various lotions and creams, purchase gourmet food items like Ben and Jerry's ice cream, take home a frozen pizza, or buy a balloon bouquet for a sweetheart.

I had already discovered another business venture for Buckwheat even before I had met him. When Cindy was explaining the various workings of the cabin to us, she pointed to the bookshelf in the living room and indicated that there were books and CDs of local artists. While pursuing the offerings, I found that Buckwheat reads Robert Service poems as entertainment not only to tourists but the locals as well. Garlan has recently discovered on Cindy's bookshelves the mystery novels of both John Straley and Dana Stabenow as well as James Michener's *Alaska.* He has gone already from a somewhat lukewarm reader to an avid one.

As we board the train on this day, I wonder if I'll display my usual fear of heights as the narrow gauge train climbs the steep mountainside on its twice-daily ascent to White Pass. I hope I can keep myself under control since I won't have the usual freedom to scream "slow down" at the engineer as I do with Garlan as we drive up steep mountain climbs in the car. Even the old sixteen millimeter movie camera on our honeymoon in 1965 captured a frowning, unhappy bride at the summit of Pike's Peak. I was still trying to recover from the frightful drive up the mountain and vowed to myself that if I could just get down safely I'd never do such a rash act again. Mississippi Delta women don't see mountains that much, or even curves.

We begin the train ride up with the usual narration by one of the train guides who tells us primarily about the Gold Rush expeditions in 1898 after the one-hundred-ten-mile train route was completed. While I'm interested in the original construction, I'm more interested in what happened during the war since Pop was the commander of Company A of the 770th Railway Operating Battalion.

My mind tunes out the narrator's stories temporarily as I try to imagine what his life was like from 1943–1944 when he was here. I need to understand what the Army hoped to achieve.

I knew some of the basics already—that the United States was afraid the Japanese would attack this vulnerable area since Japan was a mere 650 miles from Alaska—the distance between St. Louis and Atlanta. And indeed they did with an attack on Dutch Harbor the year before Pop arrived. The railroad itself was in a state of disrepair, and the equipment was antiquated— every one of the engines pressed into service by the wartime emergency was left over from the gold rush era. In a mere few months, the war material hauled had increased by ten times even in the worst possible winter conditions. The winters of 1942–43 and 1943–44 contributed to the temporary closing of the line—once for ten days and again for eighteen.

For Pop personally (also a native of the Mississippi Delta), I know the cold weather must have been a tremendous adjustment. Combined with the loneliness and his age (47), I'm sure he was discouraged many of those cold days. Like most of the other servicemen, however, he was dedicated to the completion of his mission. Whatever reserves he had within him must have been called into duty. My favorite memento of this period is the photograph of him with his fellow officers and the enlisted men. He is standing upright with a slight closed-mouth smile. I know that Mam's time with him in the summer of 1944 helped make the job more bearable.

As I return to the present, I hear the narrator tell us that we have just reached the top of White Pass and that we'll be there for a few minutes while the engines are reversed so that we can travel the miles back to Skagway. She tells us we can step out onto the platform for photographs and videos of the aqua glacier lake, but there's no time to disembark. Besides, she says, we're also in Canadian territory now, and we can't get off for immigration reasons.

I'm surprised that we're on the peak already, and I've been totally calm as we ascended the steep passes, crossed through two dark tunnels, viewed the rushing rapids thousands of feet below us, marveled at several waterfalls, including Pitchfork Falls (from Mam's postcard), and glanced down at the snake-like valley below us. I somehow feel the presence of Pop in a soothing, calming way—as if to say to me (although he died when I was twelve, and I have a few memories of him but not as many as of Mam), "You're here; you're finally here. Now you know about The Skagway Connection. Perhaps you should whisper it to the winds, but then, perhaps it should remain our secret."

I think about the definition of the word *railroad,* "a road composed of parallel steel-rails supported by ties and providing a track for trains." Pop essentially dedicated himself for all of his career to keeping those roadbeds safe and well repaired so that the thousands of people (as well as the thousands of pounds of equipment) could arrive safely to their destination.

The sacrifice for him (and the others) was monumental. I'm sure every day he was gruffly barking out orders to his men the way he did in the Mississippi Delta, as he worked for the Illinois Central Railroad. My favorite cartoon in Mam's memorabilia shows a gigantic Alaskan bear in the center devouring a fish. One of his soldiers had evidently given it to him since it was marked, "Capt. Rogers." The bear is in the midst of the snow-peaked mountains of Skagway, the totem pole is on the left-hand side of the cartoon, and the water with a small boat is visible in the background. The tiniest figure of all is a small soldier, all in black, with a host of fellow soldiers shadowed in the background. The soldier is saluting the bear.

Chapter Twenty-three
Heritage

Many years ago today, September 25, 1979, Mama and Nelson walked the boardwalks here in Skagway as one of the scheduled stops on their Princess cruise to Alaska. I'm sure she was thinking of her own Mama as well as Judy and me while she was here. In the travelogue of her experience on the cruise, called "My Trip to Alaska," she reports that she tried to find the house where Mam and Pop lived during the war but was unable to locate it.

Garlan and I have been more successful (at least we think so). We found the old black and white photograph of Mam sitting in her Jeep, Lillian, and paid attention especially to the background, where one could see the house and just a tip of a mountain. The house was a small frame one with two windows and a door in front; the shape of the roof was a small, upside-down V. Since the town of Skagway has changed little in population or housing since the war, we are quickly able to cover the twenty-two-block-long and four-street-wide location on our search.

Although the house looks slightly different from 1944, the house at 131 Main, occupied by the Moodys, appears to be the one. Like most houses from this era, it has been added onto toward the back. We'll go back a bit later and get photographs for our own memorabilia.

I think a lot these days about the importance of houses to

us as women. Many literary theorists have discussed this idea recently with the thesis that women's private spaces are represented by their houses with their warm kitchens and perhaps scents of apple pie and cinnamon, contrasted to men's public places, represented by their important jobs in the community. I tend to think, though, that women's private spaces contain the center of what our children learn and remember of us—especially regarding our faith. In 2 Timothy 1:5, Paul says, "I call to remembrance the genuine faith that is in you, which dwelt first in your grandmother, Lois and your mother Eunice, and I am persuaded is in you also."

With Mam, the center of her locus was her spacious kitchen, where she spent most of her time, it seemed. Sometimes I wonder where I get my love of making homemade cinnamon rolls or cakes and sharing them with others. Then I remember Mam. She was always "cooking a cake," as she used to say, to take to a shut-in along with a *Home Life* (a monthly magazine with inspirational stories and daily devotions). On several occasions as a child in the summer with Mam and Pop, I remember going with her to see Edna and her little Shirley. Edna was a single mother who barely got by and was living in a tiny shotgun house in Tutwiler. Whenever we'd go with the cake and a *Home Life*, little Shirley would be playing with her button collection. We'd sit on her bed in the living room and look at all the shapes and sizes and colors imaginable. Even old Mrs. Daniels down the street, who was an elitist when she first moved to Tutwiler, got treated to a cake and a *Home Life* after she had surgery one time. After that, she and Mam became the best of friends, exchanging visits frequently.

With Mama, the center of her private space was her bedroom. She was always exhausted from working her split shift through the years, so we couldn't hope for many homebaked goodies from the kitchen, although occasionally, especially on rainy Sunday afternoons, she would go to the kitchen and make peanut butter fudge for us (she couldn't afford any pecans to go in it). Otherwise, she lay in her bed resting whenever she could. She'd often call Judy and me to come in and bring her a glass of iced tea or a cup of coffee, depending on the season and the time of day. While we were there, she'd say, "Sing to me; I want to hear you sing." Judy had a relatively good singing voice, but I always felt embarrassed by my lack of being able to carry a tune. Nonetheless, we would obey and sing some of her favorite hymns, such as "I Come to the Garden Alone" or "The Old Rugged Cross." She'd try to keep the lines of communication open because, after the hymns, she'd want to know what was going on in our lives as well as tell us what she was thinking about. This practice continued until her death in 1993. By that time her grandchildren occasionally didn't quite understand why they were excluded from these intimate conversations, but Mama would always say, "Excuse us, but I need to talk to my girls alone."

As I've tried to evaluate in recent years the heritage from Mama, I would say there are at least three pillars. The first is the heritage of faith. We knew, like Daddy, she was always a seeker and a searcher for Truth. I think she came close to finding it when she and Nelson moved to Seattle and joined a small community church in Des Moines.

"These people really do practice what they believe. For all my life I've looked for such a church—where the people are real," she'd say in one of our "girl conferences." We were happy for her and happy that she had chosen to show to us the importance of prayer, Bible reading, and church fellowship early on in our lives when the temptation would certainly have been to sleep late after working until one o'clock on a Saturday night at the restaurant.

The second heritage is that, because of her, both Judy and I are strong, independent women. We learned from her that a woman can do anything she chooses. We lived in a limitless world. I spent most of my childhood being embarrassed that I came from a broken home since I was certainly in the minority in the 1950s. As a sixth grader I had to read the portrait of an ideal woman as described in Proverbs 31 at a mother-daughter tea. Afterward, my teacher complimented Mama on raising such a fine daughter who, of all things, had come from a divorced home. Now I know that it was precisely those experiences that made me who I am today.

My final heritage, and one that I value greatly, is the love for books and movies. Perhaps it was escapism for her (and for me as well), but I remember the *Reader's Digest Condensed*

Books that lined the shelves of our home (she didn't have the time or the money for the unabridged versions). Movies (and popcorn) were ways to add light to an otherwise dreary existence.

As I reflect upon the ideal biblical woman, I realize that Mam was pictured in verse twenty, "She extends her hand to the poor. Yes, she reaches out her hands to the needy." I think even Mam would say about Mama, v. 29, "Many daughters have done well, but you excel them all." Yes, public places are fine—but so are the private spaces of our mothers.

Chapter Twenty-four
"Tell Me the Old, Old Story"

Just before leaving the cabin for the church service at First Presbyterian Church here in Skagway, I slip the old church bulletin, yellowed with age and stains, from the same church into my purse. I had just retrieved it moments earlier from Mam's scrapbook during the war. It is dated June 6, 1943, a year before she arrived in Skagway to spend the months of August, September, and October of 1944 with Pop. I assume it must have been his practice also to attend the church even in her absence. I admit I'm surprised a bit since most research studies show women generally to be the religious ones in a family (but then again, it was wartime).

I know the church is an old one. When we arrive, we are handed a new bulletin listing the order of worship. I flip it over to the back side and read the history of this church. As many business ventures in Skagway in 1897 arose to meet the demands of the seekers of gold in the Klondike, so was there also the demand for a church. Rev. R. N. Dickey, a Canadian Presbyterian minister, first built a union church to encompass seven denominations, but the Presbyterians took over the ministry a couple of years later. This church building was built by the Methodists in 1901 but became the home of the Presbyterians in 1917.

The bulletin indicates that the church is the same as it was when constructed. Original equipment includes opera seats, ceiling, and lights. Some eighteen years ago the exterior was even restored to its original colors.

I see the order of the service has changed little in the years between 1943 and 1999; there is still a musical prelude, call to worship, hymns, offering, sermon, and benediction. There are, however, a few changes, such as having a children's moment where the children come to the front of the church for a story usually filled with objects they can see and touch to make the Scripture clearer to them. I also notice that the new bulletin contains no specific prayer for servicemen as it did in 1943.

As I finish reading the bulletin from cover to cover, I begin to focus on the surroundings, and I feel as if I've returned to my past in the 1950s and am competing once again with Billy Bruister to learn Psalms 24. To the left is an antique-looking wooden banner that lists the hymn numbers for today's service; to the right is a matching one but this time with captions: number in attendance, offering, budget needs for offering. To the right is also a large picture of Jesus, which we adults and children have always found comforting. It's the one with the sheep; He holds one lovingly in His hands while holding his large staff beside Him.

As in 1943, the church is without a pastor. An interim one has accepted the challenge, but he and his family will not be arriving until November. In the war, the chaplain served as the pastor because of the absence of the minister.

As the service begins, the small choir begins to sing the familiar hymns that are old, old ones from the past. One of the choir members is an aging, white-haired woman whose name is Barbara, and she plays a dulcimer. After the choir sits down, she is left alone and begins to strum and sing, "Do, Lord." I smile and think of Mam since I've heard her sing that song so many times in her big kitchen in Tutwiler as she prepared those three daily meals, cooking all the dishes on high heat as she sang. I think to myself that both of these women are definitely going to be remembered (as the hymn lyrics go) in heaven for their faithfulness here on earth.

I wait for the traditional male member of the congregation to come forward and give the sermon. Instead, I'm surprised and gratified to see that a woman, Sheryl, has been chosen to give the sermon (never at a traditional Southern Baptist Church). She has selected one-liners from several hymns that have been meaningful to her through the years. The first one comes from page one of the hymnbook: "Joyful, Joyful, We Adore Thee." The one-liner she focuses on is "center of unbroken praise" located in the second verse. She speaks of how often it is in difficult circumstances such as illness, loneliness, and financial reversals for us continually to praise God. We then sing the verse from which the one-liner has been taken. After several songs, interspersed by Sheryl's insightful comments, we conclude this portion of the service with the one-liner, "all I have needed He hath provided." I think again to myself of the absolute, unyielding Truth of this line. In spite of poverty, a difficult childhood, whatever, God has provided for all of my needs, both physically and spiritually.

After the traditional chorus "There Is a Redeemer," we adjourn to the Recreation Hall for a time of fellowship. As I pass the old bulletin around the table for the current members to examine, I'm surprised that one of the old timers, John, actually remembers the story of Miss Margaret Johnston, who was the organist in 1943. He goes on to tell me she married one of the servicemen who was stationed in Skagway during the war. He has no memory, though, of the interim chaplain, A. Mack.

I sit at the table with my new friend, Margaret (the sister of one of my friends at home). I realize that she has needs that God will have to provide for her over the next few weeks. She explains that, for the first time in four years, her house is empty since her grandson, Jamie, has just gone into the service. He has lived with her during his high school years (as I did with Mam), and now there's no one's footsteps to listen for. She tells me of the lean years here in Skagway after the railway had to shut down for a few years. Vernon and she collected unemployment ($500 a month) and supported three children on that. The first month they received it they called in a serviceman to fill up their old oil tank for winter. The bill was $500. She's also anticipating surgery within the next weeks in Seattle. She's weepy with good reason, I think, but I am assured that God will meet her needs as well through this difficult time. I tell her that I will pray for her and I will help her in any way I can after her surgery.

As we leave and begin to think of the new week before us, I pray that we will continue to remember to tell the old, old story—of Jesus and His love. I think the sentiments for all of us as men and women in 1943 or 1999—whether we're young or old, weak or strong—are close to that of Ignatius Loyala (printed on the front of the 1943 bulletin): "Teach us, O Lord, to serve Thee as Thou deservest; to give, and not to count the cost; to fight, and not to heed the wounds; to toil, and not to seek for rest; to labor, and to ask for no reward save that of knowing that we do Thy will; through Jesus Christ our Lord."

Chapter Twenty-five
Museums and Man

As we pass by the door of the Trail of '98 Skagway Museum, it is September 27. We notice by the sign on the door that we have a few brief days yet to tour it since it will be closing for the season on the 30th. We realize we must get back tomorrow.

The next day we once again marvel at the front exterior of the museum since over 20,000 pieces of natural wood, instead of finished wood slabs, were used to finish off the building. I admit we're rushing a bit since I have an appointment at one o'clock at the library to check my email from home. We know it's a small museum, essentially a natural museum with artifacts from the past one hundred years as well as photographs, and we assure ourselves that we'll have sufficient time.

Ella Sullivan, the museum host, tells us that we can sit and watch two twenty-five-minute video slide presentations of the history of the town before we tour if we'd like. We go over to the viewing area and see the titles of the two offerings; one focuses on the gold rush days, but the other is entitled "Skagway at War." We know immediately which one we'll insert first.

The slides of the war years here reveal that the town's main street (Broadway) and the surrounding area have changed little in the past years. We are surprised, though, to see that the White Pass and Yukon Railroad tracks ran directly through the main street with its buildings lining each side.

The narrator takes us mentally through the incredible task of building the Alaskan Highway in a mere eight months during the war in spite of the harsh winter weather. We sit up straight in our seats as he begins to discuss the railroad repair and upgrade by the 770th Railway Operating Battalion. Soon the slide of the officers is shown, and we see Pop's face grinning rather widely this time on the first row center of the small group. We know we'll have to purchase the video and take it home for Judy to see.

Our time has gone so quickly, and we rush off to the library but ask the museum host if she will allow us to return in a half hour or so to finish the tour. She assents and seems pleased that we asked.

When we return, we enter into the large room filled with numerous reminders of the past. We take our time and read many of the explanations and captions. On the final lap of the museum, we see a Victorian woman mannequin within her domain—the house. Once again we wonder about the type of woman who would choose willingly to leave the comforts of civilization to live in this still-untamed wilderness. We pick up a free printed excerpt from Cynthia Brackett Driscoll's book *One Woman's Gold Rush* for a few answers. Her answer, evidently from the story of Annie Hall Strong, is a simplistic one: wherever men are, women will follow. I wonder if it's that simple, however.

Strong gives a warning in her writings to the faint-hearted, "delicate women have no right attempting the trip. It means utter collapse. Those who love luxury, comfort and ease would better remain at home." She then goes on to list all the clothes and bedding a woman would do well to bring for her new life in Alaska—with just one good dress being listed.

I tend to think that there were other strong motivating factors for women to risk life and limb to come here. Some of the heartiest no doubt were looking for that big vein of gold for themselves, not necessarily being willing to share it with anyone else. Others in the world's oldest profession came for new business, and they would certainly get a lot of it. The male miners came up by boat from Seattle in search of the elusive gold. They also came south again to celebrate their strike with many drinks in the Skagway saloons or to bemoan their fate if their gold pans had sifted fool's gold instead. Others came for missionary purposes since the Salvation Army arrived shortly after the gold rush began, and many souls here were, no doubt, in need of salvation.

As we leave we notice an exhibit of the Alaska Native man who is fully equipped for hunting caribou. His mask is made from walrus tusk, and his clothes from the natural hides of the animals. His weapons have been fashioned from stones or from whale bone. I was instantly reminded that these men lived completely from the land with no long list of supplies being handed to them, nor disclaimers given, for life in this climate. He, by instinct and tribal teachings from his family, learned to use all that nature has provided for survival.

As we leave the museum, Robin, who is another host for

the museum, confides that we should return for yet another
visit tomorrow.

"Ella knows so many interesting stories which she can
tell you about Skagway. Now that the tourists are gone, I'm
sure she'd love to do it."

The next day we enter the museum for the third time, and as
Robin suggested, we ask Ella for a private tour. As we again view
the exhibits, I ask her about her own life as a woman here today—
one hundred years later. Since we've met so few people actually
from Alaska (most are from the lower 48), we are almost surprised when she says she is a native.

"Actually, I was born in Haines (one hour by ferry), but my
husband and I settled here in Skagway. We raised our two children here, who are now in their forties. They still live here in
town. My husband has passed on."

"What's kept you here?" I ask.

"I guess it's that winters are so much fun around here, and
the people are so close. You know you can always count on any
of them. If there's ever any trouble in your life, you know they'll
stick up for you. We might fight and gossip a bit, but it's like a
big family. In the winter we have time for crafts, and the lodge
meetings and snowmobiling. We have the Victorian Christmas
celebration." She goes on and on with the list of activities and
the town's assets.

I think to myself, "I'm glad I asked."

And as I meditate upon her words, I think she's right: it

is about community—within the town, the family, and the culture. John Donne said it best in his meditation, "No man (or woman, I also add) is an island."

Chapter Twenty-six
Integrity and Illusions

This morning, on the second of October, we drive north toward the Yukon Territory in Canada. Since Mam and Pop spent a month together there in 1944, I'm anxious to see how much it's changed from the photographs and postcards from the scrapbook. Will it be like the Yukon portrayed in one of my favorite radio shows as a child, "Sergeant Preston of the Yukon and His Dog Named York," where the heroes mush through deep piles of snow on their husky-led sleds in pursuit of criminals?

We have already heard from the locals that it has some of the modern American fast food restaurants, such as McDonald's and Pizza Hut, but we suspect that, like Skagway, the changes have been minimal through the years.

We drive through Main Street downtown and see that indeed it appears much the same as in the past. We decide to take a quick trip through MacBride Museum, and find that its exhibits focus on the gold rush and life in the early Yukon cabins. Since Jack London did most of his writing in this area, I'm surprised to see nothing about him. One of the main streets into town, however, is named the Robert Service Road in honor of the poet. One room contains exhibits of stuffed wildlife of several species.

I'm longing to leave the world of reality and see a movie. We ask one of the shopgirls downtown for directions to the Yukon Theater. We pay in Canadian money, buy Diet Pepsi's, and sit down to watch the latest Hollywood release filmed recently in Alaska. It's called *Mystery, Alaska.* The portrayal of the locals there is a positive one for the most part. The plot centers on the hope for its hockey team to play the New York Rangers hockey team. Of course, the home team believes, although they're much smaller than the opponents, they can still have that hometown advantage since they are better skaters, and the competition will be on a pond rather than a professional ice rink. It's a controversial proposal, however, and at a town meeting, the judge (played by Burt Reynolds) argues against the game. Essentially, his speech centers on the fact that Mystery has always had its integrity and illusions, and he doesn't want to chance losing them. The opposition argues, "Where's the integrity if you don't even try?"

Although it's just an average film of a David vs. Goliath genre, it does once again show the close community spirit in this state. It also shows how difficult life is for the women in Alaska, but the message is that the women stay for no other reason than their men, who are somehow more rugged than the average man in the lower 48.

In my mind, I'm trying to determine where reality is—or if it's ever possible to know in a fictional presentation of another place. Is this film an accurate snapshot of the true grit of Alaskans, or are they more like those in John Sayles' recent movie, also filmed here, entitled *Limbo*? It's much darker than *Mystery.* Sayles' characters are all losers who have come to

Alaska, or stayed here, either because they're bad seeds or are running from their pasts. The lead characters include the town's handyman, who suffers from guilt because he survived a boating accident while the others on his fishing boat drowned, a down-and-out singer who's constantly choosing the wrong men, and her daughter, who inflicts injuries on herself because of her unhappiness. After the three become shipwrecked in a remote location, Sayles gives us an open ending. As a plane comes into focus, the screen goes blank, and the credits are run. The plane will either be piloted by an enemy who has come to kill them because they know too much about a drug deal gone wrong, or a friend who will save them. The ending is disturbing because it invites us to ask these questions regarding the fate of the characters: Would it be better for them to go on as losers, creating even more unhappiness for themselves? Realistically, would it be possible for them to change and be able to make a decent life for themselves after all? Or the worst question of all, why not end their miserable lives now? In a sense, the viewer becomes God because he or she interprets and creates a true postmodern ending.

In real life, as we all know, the underdog doesn't always win, and Sergeant Yukon doesn't always capture the fugitives with his dog named York. But essentially, I can never be as dark as Sayles; I tend to agree more with Churchill—that we should "Never give in. Never give in." I'll keep my integrity and illusions if possible.

Chapter Twenty-seven
Radio Days

I've loved radio from my earliest days, and now in Skagway, I'm returning to my first love—not by choice but by necessity.

The evening we arrived, now a month ago, Cindy announced there was one television channel here on the hill—Alaska Rural Communications System. While there was cable in town, its appearance hadn't made it up to Dyea Road.

Once one has been married for thirty-four years, the subtexts don't have to be practiced a lot. Garlan and I both looked at each other in astonishment.

"How can we ever make it here for three whole months with one TV channel!" we communicated without words.

I know I was thinking, "We might have to take the ferry home even earlier than we thought."

After all, we've grown so spoiled with our choices at home on cable. Some would even think our fifty channels are antiquated, since they have satellite systems offering as many as five hundred channels. We wondered which of the major networks we'd be forced into watching—NBC, ABC, or CBS. We soon discovered that ARCS offers a variety of programming.

The first morning, these two news junkies were saying, "Thank God," to each other as we realized we would get two hours of the "Today Show" each weekday morning. We began to adjust to seeing a few of our favorites but at odd times for us, used to the Central Time Zone. CBS Sunday Morning is on at six o'clock, for example. I know we could always attempt to locate Cindy's instruction booklet for the VCR and truly learn to preset the clock, but we haven't been able to discover it yet.

Very soon an announcement appeared across the screen warning us viewers that, because of a sun outage (we have no idea what that is), television reception would be affected. The next morning we saw the results—a loud buzz and a distorted picture. For the next two days we checked out one video after another but resisted the Ben and Jerry's gourmet ice cream, deluxe pizzas, and freshly popped corn to comfort us in our dilemma. When the reception cleared finally, we discovered the programmers had an unusual sense of humor evidently. Just as we were poised to receive the latest NFL scores, the program would cut away to another channel, or we'd be up for seeing Farrah Fawcett on the Dave Letterman show only, to lose out to a reality-based TV show.

We finally tried the radio. There we discovered a local PRI (Public Radio International) station. It does offer a variety of programming and the favorites that we've always enjoyed as we commuted from our jobs each day—"All Things Considered," "Click and Clack" for Garlan, and local news.

We started to remember together when radios were the source of family togetherness in the evenings as families across America sat around the now-antique Philco. Who can ever forget Woody Allen's touching scene in his film *Radio Days* when a child was being rescued from the bottom of a well? Hour by hour, the families listened to the dramatic reports of the rescue, only to be devastated by the news that she was dead when brought to the surface. The father of the young boy in the film realizes that one truly needs to love and value a child.

Personally, I remembered those long hours on a Sunday afternoon lying in the bed with Judy beside me, listening and eating oranges.

It's a nostalgic vision of the past, I admit, in our modern society. I guess I yearn, though, for a new and revolutionary invention for the new millennium, which might bring us back to that close sense of family once again.

Chapter Twenty-eight
Jack London and Me

It's a beautiful sunny day on October 20, and we drive up on the Klondike Highway once again toward Whitehorse. This time we have two guests, Garlan's dad and sister, who have just arrived from Wichita for a week's visit. We are anxious for them to see this spectacular scenery. It's even more than we hoped it would be for them—each peak of the mountain reveals an ever slowly cascading white robe that has its origins as a queen's crown of pure white. It has fallen in velvety folds about her waist and has now ended about her ankles. Jack London would be suspicious about the weather, but we're from the sunny South (or midwest) and drive on, taking no thought for the morrow, reveling in the sights that nature has provided us this day.

We eat, shop for Yukon souvenirs for the nieces, see a movie *(Random Hearts)*, and stay overnight at the somewhat elegant Westmark Hotel downtown. All is well until we awaken for our return trip down the Klondike to Skagway to see that two inches or so of snow have fallen during the night. We flatlanders begin to panic as we think of the slowly winding highway ascending to the top of White Pass and remember the impassable pass photographs from Mam's World War II album.

Nevertheless, we know we must go. We do everything we can to prepare for the trip (as recommended by the locals). We have plenty of warm clothes, a tankful of gas, candles, water, and even emergency oatmeal raisin cookies, should we become stranded. As an extra precaution, Garlan throws a sandbag into the trunk of the car along with our weighty luggage. He stops at the Petro Canada tire shop and buys clip-on tire chains just in case. We've already checked with both the Royal Canadian Police and the customs agent at the Canadian border for the go-ahead. We've heard that sometimes the gates will be down along the highway if it becomes impassable, forcing the traveler to return either to Whitehorse or Skagway. I begin to relate to the key characters in Jack London's short story "To Build a Fire."

During my days as a junior high teacher in the mid-seventies, I taught the story many times, but I have to admit the circumstances always seemed a bit strange to us Southerners. Surely, in similar circumstances, I've always thought we'd be much more savvy than the protagonist, who doesn't heed the advice from all the locals. "Don't go out into this well-below zero weather; it's too dangerous," they essentially tell him.

Of course, he ignores their advice and sets off with his Alaskan dog by his side, convinced he knows better than they. After a dip into icy waters and finding his wet matches totally useless, he freezes to death while the dog, using eons of survival instinct, trots calmly back to the warm camp.

For this trip, I'm determined to be calm, however, and let my husband do the driving, although I've insisted on sitting up front in the passenger seat, ejecting my eighty-two-year-old father-in-law so that I can help Garlan watch the highway. My need for control uncovers itself once again. I know there are poles for guidelines on each side of the highway to assist drivers on white-out days of driving.

We creep along ever so slowly and find that, especially on curves and the steep mountain climbs, the road crew has been along just moments earlier to sand the roadbed. I decide to enjoy the view. Of course, this time of fall in the Yukon reveals that the leaves on the cottonwoods or aspens have dropped away until spring. We see the heavy snow wetly clinging to the boughs of the evergreens. The road is totally snow covered, and the flakes begin to fall even more heavily until it becomes a challenge to see the road ahead.

We cross a bridge and see a lone coyote pacing slowly on the snow-covered banks as if even he isn't quite sure how this surprising event has happened so quickly in the night. We see a snowshoe rabbit on the right of the car. He seems to be having the opposite reaction; he seems to be saying to himself, "It's about time. I've put up with all the reds and golden colors of the fall so long. Now I can hop about enjoying the time of year for which I was created—invisible to my enemies."

We stop briefly at Carcross, a First Nations settlement, for aspirin at the Shell station since Garlan has a headache. The travelers inside are sharing stories of their treks either northward or southward. The warmth inside overwhelms us as we enter, along with the scents of cigarette smoke and deli fried chicken.

Soon we arrive at the Canadian customs, just twenty miles

from Skagway, and are excited to find that the gate is up, and we can proceed to our destination. As we pass the American customs office fourteen miles down the mountain, we find the winter storm has disappeared. Skagway has only rain. Cindy's place has never looked as good to us. We build a fire ourselves with dry matches, pop popcorn, and sip hot chocolate the rest of the afternoon thinking of Jack London one hundred years ago and the natural instinct of the animals who have the ability to survive year after year during these brutal winter days to come.

Chapter Twenty-nine
Frozen in Their Tracks

On this Sunday afternoon in late October, the sun has scampered out for the briefest of moments during the church service as if to give its approval to the churchgoers at First Presbyterian. We have noticed it before; the days can be overwhelmingly gray all six days before, yet every Sunday we've been in Skagway, we see the playful sun peeping through the stained glass windows, perhaps to say to us, "Lighten up a bit; enjoy the day, which I have made for you."

The four of us (Garlan, his dad, his sister, and I) decide to do just that after lunch. The adventure this day will be to drive down Dyea Road, where we live, to its very end, which we understand from the sign is eight miles after the pavement stops. We have some history for the old gold rush town, which is no longer in existence in Dyea, housing today not a thriving community with fifty-two bars but just a campground. We know its story: On April 3, 1898, in the midst of the excitement in the Klondike, an avalanche killed the town's population. We also know there's a cemetery there for us to view.

We're somewhat leery of the drive down the mountain because we've already witnessed the repair trucks with their grinding gears as they climb the mountain. Their trucks have been down the road to clear several mud slides a few times already. The weather here, being a coastal climate, is always damp. I don't relish the idea of being buried by a mudslide any more than I would an avalanche. I'm so bored, however, with staying inside the cabin that I am more than agreeable to the Dyea trip.

As we wind slowly down the mud and gravel road, which keeps getting more and more narrow, I find myself losing the patience I had gained from the Whitehorse snow excursion.

"Garlan, stop going down the left of the road. Someone may actually be coming toward us!" I holler.

"I'm just trying to miss these potholes," he calmly replies.

An ensuing discussion follows between Garlan and his dad about the likely need to purchase new shocks when we get home in January. I know the battle is lost, so I settle in, uncomfortably trying to avoid looking at the soft shoulder immediately to my left with its concurrent drop into icy, Arctic waters seemingly a few inches away.

We finally reach level ground and discover a wildlife refuge that was totally unexpected. Several signs indicate the various animals we will likely see from our vantage point. I immediately spot a bald eagle sitting on an old stump across the water and scramble for my video camera.

We come to the Dyea Cemetery cutoff and follow the ever worsening road for several hundred feet until we find it. As we emerge from the protection of the car, we experience an eerie quiet and an enveloping scent of pine. There might not have been gold for these folks, but there was definitely frankincense and myrrh. I am immediately struck by the comment on the sign which says that some seventy or so people were killed that day in April, ironically Palm Sunday, some one hundred years ago. Many were frozen in running positions by the descending avalanche.

I've always wondered about someone who could be frozen in his or her tracks by fear. I think about other people who have experienced a similar fate. One, of course, is Lot's wife who glanced back at the cities of Sodom and Gomorrah and became a pillar of salt. At least one modern poet, Ana Akhmatova, has questioned whether Lot's wife disobeyed God's command overtly or was simply yearning for what she was leaving behind. In either case, the result was the same.

Who can ever explain the deaths of countless individuals through the disasters of nature? Many still believe in the punishment of God for ungodly living. Scientists, of course, use the argument that conditions in the environment were just right for such a disaster to take place. I tend to think that one simply needs to be ready for death. Until he or she has confronted that giant, no living can take place.

Chapter Thirty
Morning Rituals

Thoreau had his personal morning rituals as he lived on Walden Pond for his two-year experiment. His language was often full of Eastern mystical chants and experiences related to the coming of the day, rather unlike the typical Western writers of his time—more full of hope for equality and the democratic spirit. Garlan and I too have our morning rituals here in Skagway relating to the new day.

I flip on the kitchen light in the tiny galley kitchen of our cabin and begin to make the coffee while dressed in my long johns (since we don't have any near neighbors, just as Thoreau didn't, it doesn't matter how we dress). The light seems to be a signal for two year-round residents of this two-acre plot of ground—the small squirrel and the bluejay—to prepare for the surprise of the morning feast.

Just to ensure that I have noticed their presence, both vie for my attention in the kitchen windows. Bluejay seems to prefer the side window as he rushes very close to the light and retreats hastily. Ground squirrel, on the other hand, is more forceful in his begging. He runs back and forth across the outside seal of the window, frequently pausing to sit up on his hind legs and make clicking noises.

I pause from my own attention to the oatmeal boiling impatiently on the stovetop in order to heed their requests.

"Okay, okay, I've got something for you today. Just be patient, please!" I say good-naturedly.

The surprise of the morning feast is that these two never quite know what leftovers I'll provide for their breakfast. So far they've enjoyed walnuts, pistachio nuts, homemade bread, soy pancakes (I'm sure they didn't find those very tasty since we didn't either), Honey Nut Cheerios, and cheese muffins. Today I look about the pantry and find two leftover fortune cookies from our recent Chinese meal in Whitehorse.

"What the heck," I say to myself as I bite into the plastic wrap.

As usual, I crumble the offerings into bite-size portions (I wouldn't want one of them to eat too quickly), and the fortunes within the cookies fall out onto the breakfast table. I place the crumbs outside for the squirrel and bluejay, sit in my window seat, and watch them come to the table for the feast. At first they were very competitive for the crumbs; now they have decided to share, realizing there's enough for both.

The squirrel tends to eat one bite and rush off with a bite in his mouth (I assume he has a nest under the fall leaves close by in which to store food for the coming winter season). The bluejay usually swallows several bites before he flies away, only to return quickly for more. The squirrel scampers away; the bluejay then sees his opportunity to eat. Occasionally, they face off with the squirrel chattering and the bluejay squawking fiercely.

"Patience, patience, boys," again I say.

I glance over at the fortunes lying before me on the breakfast table, take one to Garlan, who's watching the news on TV, and open mine to read.

"Nature, time, and patience are the three great physicians," I read.

"Yes," I say to Confucius, "that's very true, but I'd like to add one additional physician to your list—God."

As I reflect on the truth of this statement, I realize that all of these physicians have been monumental influences for me during my five-month sabbatical thus far. I gaze out upon the snow-capped mountain peaks also outside my window. Every morning they change. Sometimes they are draped with a fine fog, which lifts as the day lightens, revealing their faithful guard of evergreens and even golden cottonwood and aspen leaves in mid-fall. Some days in this coastal environment we even get a glimpse of the sun's rays on the peaks as if they are illuminating the glory of several pure-haired old women dressed in varying shades of green and canary, not purple.

I realize that, as far as time, I've never had an extended period in which to reflect and come to terms with life's challenges. An abundance of time has caused me to look within and to reconcile. What is time commonly for most people who are consumed with careers and family? It is a fleeting vapor, as the book of James reminds us; our life is "a vapor, that appeareth for a little time, and then vanisheth away." Putting time into slow motion, as I've been able to do recently, has been invaluable.

Like the squirrel and the bluejay, I often find myself impatient in so many areas of my life. I long to be more consistent in my moods and have more patience with the people who are the most important to me.

Confucius and the other wise teachers of the ancient Chinese world almost got it right. They missed it, however, by not having a clear idea as to the nearness of God for each one of us. They believed in a rather nebulous idea of Him: The deity was seen as an anthropomorphic divinity, or a natural and moral force, or a collective of ancestral spirits. I'm thankful for the Western religious tradition, which sees Him as personal, caring, and loving.

"Thoreau, I hope your meditations at Walden Pond were as helpful as mine have been in Skagway," I say to myself as I put the oatmeal on our table. Morning rituals are good. I look forward to the day when God "preparest a table before me ... anointest my head with oil," for I will know fully then that "my cup runneth over."

Chapter Thirty-one
Give Me Light, or Give Me Chocolate

Since I've been in Alaska for the past seven weeks, I've noticed a lot of social problems. Everywhere I go—to the library restroom, to the grocery store, on the TV—I see evidences of them. Now that November has arrived, and although not officially declared as the dead of winter, most of the locals seem resigned that the windy, rainy or snowy days are here for a full six-month period, or until the first tourist ship of the season arrives once again at the port of Skagway. Already I've seen several television features reminding Alaskans of the dangers and warning signs of SAD (Seasonal Affective Disorder). Evidently, this diagnosed disease is akin to clinical depression in that certain individuals react negatively to the decreasing amounts of light during the winter months. If one begins to sleep much more than usual, and craves carbohydrates, he or she is likely to have SAD and will need special high-dose light treatments in order to recover.

So far I've heard two direct references to SAD. One was from the local disk jockey who said his wife frequently screams out to him, "Give me light, or give me chocolate!" Another young wife in church yesterday asked for special prayer, indicating that winter was always very difficult for her.

I think if I were a resident here year round, I'd also be a candidate for SAD. I do miss the sunny South when the wind gusts hover at 70 mph., the rain falls in great masses of streams on the tin roof of the cabin for 48 hours straight, and the power outages become longer and more frequent. According to the radio announcer, if one even chooses to go out, he or she should watch carefully for fallen, and even flying, debris. The ferry for home comes just once a week, and even it can be delayed because of the high tides. The only highway to the north—White Pass on the Klondike—is closed. I've already decided that I could not have survived the gold rush days here one hundred years ago. Life is hard enough here now.

If the threat of SAD and the weather isn't enough, there's also the child and spousal abuse posters and public service announcements everywhere. They are in such abundance in Alaska that the problem must be a severe one as well. I can bet that in a lot of households in winter, one doesn't do anything but sit around and either drink at home or at the local bar downtown. I've been there in childhood and know there's a definite connection between liquor and abuse.

Sadly, the news also reports a gigantic increase, two and one-half times, in the number of children who have to be placed in foster homes from September to October. In this instance, however, there's another culprit to consider in addition to SAD, weather, and drink—the receipt of the Alaskan permanent fund check. This money seems to be unique in that every resident receives a dividend in October from investments the state has made. This year it was a record $1,770. Social workers believe the rise in the need for foster housing for children comes about because the once-a-year appearance of this money allows parents simply to abandon their children in search of a good time.

Unfortunately, the state of Alaska isn't the only one that has to deal with these gigantic demons of social unrest. In Arkansas, the problems, I believe, stem more from poverty than SAD, weather, or other factors. Until we can, as a nation, learn why we do the things we do and truly adopt the idea of compassion, we will make no progress toward solving the other problems that plague us.

Chapter Thirty-two
Like a Grounded Eagle

We feel as if we've almost become locals since our arrival in Skagway two months ago. Tonight we casually sit at the ferry terminal, glancing out at the rolling ocean (somewhat calm for "the home of the north wind"), and waiting for the approach of the single light of the ferry. We're on our way to Haines, a mere 45 minutes away by water but hundreds of miles if we chose to go by car. I marvel once again at the Alaskan Marine Highway system, which so efficiently and tirelessly it seems, delivers hundreds of passengers, vehicles, and cargo in and out of the port towns along its route.

We've been reading and hearing about the annual Bald Eagle Festival for a while now, which has been promoted as "the largest congregation of eagles" anywhere in the world during the winter months. We're told they come because of the attraction of the menu—salmon, which have swum hundreds of miles upstream, relentlessly seeking just the right spot to lay their eggs. They know by instinct that their job in nature has been fulfilled at that time, and they are willing to sacrifice themselves to become the head of the food chain. Eagles and other wildlife then feast on their bodies. The eagles particularly, we're told, stuff themselves with the freshest salmon, just pulled from the icy waters, and then sit lazily for hours at the tops of trees to digest their food. After reading the advertising brochures, I realize, along with Dorothy in *Jerry*

Maguire, I've been had again at "hello."

After spending the night in a local motel in Haines, we arise early for our eagle viewing at the Chilkat Bald Eagle Preserve, established in 1982, at the Mile 19 marker on the highway. We've decided to forego our pretense at being locals (our Southern accents give us away anyway) and book a three-hour tour to the preserve. We'll ride an old school bus and be given some interesting facts about the habits and habitats of these magnificent creatures.

While we're waiting for our one o'clock departure, we visit the two museums in town—the Sheldon Museum and Cultural Center and the American Bald Eagle Foundation. The locals in Haines, I guess because of their rest from cruise tourists for the past six weeks, seem excited and animated again. They are extremely talkative. One of the museum guides at Sheldon tells us two interesting facts about the nature of eagles.

One is that their eyes are gold in their youth; in their mature stage their eyes are silver. We already knew about the white head appearing as the eagles age, changing from its earlier golden-brown appearance.

What fascinates me most is his story of the eagles and their eyesight. Of course, as children we learn about the penetrating eyesight of the eagles and their ability to spot prey or dangers hundreds of feet away. What we don't hear about, however, is that when their eyes are covered (in order to work with them at a clinic, for example), they become totally docile, never requiring anesthesia even for a procedure. It's as if they have developed total trust in their handlers.

We glance at our watches and hurry away, for it will be time soon for us to board the bus for our trip to the preserve. The ground and trees are snow covered here, unlike in Skagway, fitting our preconceptions of a perfect Alaskan autumn day. We know the days are short now for us—just over seven hours of daylight daily—so we know we're there at the best possible moment. The elusive sun even confirms its approval and gives us a transient moment of blue sky, which I capture with the video camera.

We see photographers everywhere along the water with their tripods, mammoth zoom lenses, and cameras facing the eagles, who are now feeding on salmon or perched in trees, digesting salmon. I decide size does matter, at least in photography, as I glance at my measly 35 mm automatic focus camera. I'm trying to be rather sophisticated, however, about not being too pushy about being first, as usual, to look through several telescopic lenses which the tour guide has set up for our close-up viewing.

My moment finally comes, and I am stunned by the apparent closeness of the first eagle who sits eating—nonchalant to all the excitement he and his friends are causing. Later, I get several views through the telescope of eagles in trees, salmon spawning in the water, and a variety of other wildlife, which have gathered together along the water.

After a couple of hours in the preserve, we head back into

town. It is only later—as we ride on the late night ferry back into Skagway—that I can meditate upon nature's lessons of the day. We sit in the front lounge, which is completely dark, to see what we can see ahead. I guess I expected the ferry to have some type of headlight like a car. Instead, there's a ghostly blackness both inside and outside the ferry. Before us, one can see only tiny lights that mark the channel. I'm startled as a spotlight eerily comes on periodically to check for unseen dangers. One time we see a flock of seagulls starboard.

I feel myself beginning to experience that old anxiety from childhood as I hear the waves lapping along the side of the boat. Like Emily Dickinson in her poem "I heard a Fly buzz—when I died—," I too "could not see to see—." I strain anyway to slice through the pervading ink of the night, knowing the dangers of mountains and ice along each side of the narrow passage that we are gliding through. I think of the movie *Titanic,* with Rose and Jack clinging to one another in the icy water. Then I remember....

The lesson of the grounded eagle begins to give me calmness. He, when confronted by unexpected darkness, simply gives himself to the power of the unseen Hand, in whose presence he resides, taking him from his current world of darkness into a healing light.

Chapter Thirty-three
"All the World's a Stage"

It's a rather foggy Alaskan evening on November 13 when I set out alone for my trek off the mountain into town. Garlan has opted to stay at the cabin for an early-to-bed evening, but as for me, I'm going to the theater. The Skagway Drama Club is presenting Thornton Wilder's production of *The Matchmaker,* which has been billed as a farce in four acts.

I've been a fan of Wilder's since my course in American drama at the University of Mississippi. We read all of his plays, which were still considered experimental drama in the early 1970s. *The Matchmaker* is the one that centers on the adventures of Horace Vandergelder in his pursuit of a wife. To assist him in his quest, he uses the services of a matchmaker, Mrs. Dolly Levi, who has already picked herself as the future wife. She doesn't tell anyone but the audience of her plan, however, and it's here that the farce begins.

I arrive early at the school where the play will be performed and sit by myself in the middle of a row. Already, as I watch the locals come in, I realize that I'm soon going to pass for one myself. I see Maxine from church, Julene and Robin from the library, and Chris from the video store.

In the minutes remaining before the curtain opens, I get sympathetic butterflies in my stomach as I think not of the predominantly high school cast but of the director, or directors in this case, since there are two.

It seems like last year to me, not twenty years ago, that I was directing plays at Shiloh Christian School. Since the school was just beginning to establish itself, I did what the locals here in Skagway do. Instead of one job, I had six. I taught, in addition to drama, English, Geography, American History, Journalism, and Bible. I actually think I preferred the variety compared to my previous teaching position where I taught one section of English six times a day.

My first big drama production was to occur in Advent shortly before the students were to get their Christmas vacation. I had a cast of seventh and eighth graders. The students worked hard with the simultaneous sets: a modern setting to stage left and a biblical one to stage right. Looking back, I am glad I hadn't read John Irving's *A Prayer for Owen Meany*; in fact it wasn't to be written for another ten years or so. The scene where Owen, because of his tiny size, plays baby Jesus is hilarious but would give a drama teacher nightmares for life. Owen has a crush on the girl who plays Mary and attempts to grab her breasts during the performance, disrupting all semblance of a smooth performance.

The concern for my play simply was to keep our "baby Jesus" safe since the mother of a six-week-old infant boy whose name was John had given us permission for him to make his stage debut. We practiced with a toy baby through dress rehearsal. At a crucial scene the night before the actual performance,

Tonya, the student playing Mary, stumbled over a hay bale—
flinging the doll baby violently to the stage floor.

My nerves for the next twenty-four hours were jangled,
and I'm sure I didn't sleep at all the night before the performance. Previously, I had thought the biggest problem might be
if the baby cried and the performers' lines were muffled.

Strangely enough, once the play began, I felt an overwhelming aura of calmness. I knew it was in God's hands
from that point on. When baby Jesus was born in the manger
and Mary held him, he simply looked up adoringly at his
mother. When she placed him in the manger, the audience
could hear a cooing sound and saw the baby waving his arms
about contentedly. At the conclusion of the play, just as we
had planned, the stable walls slipped smoothly and quietly
down, revealing a huge cross over the baby's manger spot-
lighted by a soft, red light to signify His coming sacrifice.

As the play's director, I breathed a long sigh a relief.

For the performance tonight at Skagway, I also begin to
relax and enjoy the play as the players begin. I notice from the
program that the director is also the Vandergelder character (I
don't think I could ever have nerves of steel to pull that one off).
The two lead characters are wonderful, as is the young boy who
plays Barnaby with a keen sense of comedic timing. At one
point early on in the play, Vandergelder dramatically announces,
"You're going to get a new mistress," to which Barnaby flawlessly reacts, "I can't; I'm too young." Barnaby also gets to give

the familiar moral, which we expect from Wilder's plays at the end, lest someone has witnessed the performance and still doesn't get it. Basically, for *The Matchmaker* it's that when we're at home we long for the big adventure, but when we're on the big adventure, we long for home. I relate to that and say to myself, "That's true, Wilder; that's really true."

After the performance, I always love the curtain call where everyone comes to stage front for their kudos. I know they're physically and mentally exhausted, but they all manage to enjoy the moment greatly as they get their fifteen minutes of fame.

"All the world's a stage," Shakespeare said, and what a marvelous opportunity our small schools have to nurture the talent of its future leaders.

Chapter Thirty-four
A Community Thanksgiving

On this Thanksgiving Day, we realize that we are hundreds of miles away from home and are finding it hard to get enthused about the holiday. Instead of hosting family and friends as we usually do in Siloam Springs, there will be "just the two of us" (as Will Smith sings in his popular song of a year ago). I go to the Fairway Market and languidly look at the sign that announces fresh turkeys are available in the back. I think of Garlan's mom's recipe for cranberry salad and realize that it makes enough for fifteen people at least. It's at this point that I see Dirce from church and stop to ask her about the Community Thanksgiving dinner.

"Hi, Dirce," I say, "I just wanted to ask you about the dinner this Thursday. Is it really for the community, or is it primarily for the poor and homeless?" I guess in some ways we could be considered homeless (at least being away from our home) but certainly not in the current use of the word.

"Oh, it's for everyone in the community who doesn't have another place to go. You just bring a potluck dish," she replies.

Garlan and I talk it over and decide to take two pecan pies and enjoy the meal Thanksgiving Day at the Presbyterian Church. As we go down the stairs, we see about thirty folks already gathered around the long tables that have been placed end to end banquet style. We see the interim pastor, Bob Cameron, and his wife, Mariam. After the food is blessed, Eva announces for all to come forward and get salads; after that, the hot dishes will be passed from person to person, family style.

As I sit at the table, I remember that this is not the first holiday meal that has been enjoyed in Skagway by someone in our family. Pop made sure Mam kept his Christmas Day menu of 1943 from the 770th Railway Operating Battalion in her scrapbook. As I looked at the menu recently, I noticed its cartoon cover showed Santa carrying a huge bag of food and toys through the snow as a chubby Beetle Bailey type of soldier looked on humorously. As I reviewed the menu inside, I noticed that it (like today's meal) contained all the traditional trimmings—turkey, dressing, sweet potatoes, and mincemeat pie, but it also offered the now-frowned-upon cigarettes and cigars. All of this was provided to comfort our boys in service who were also away from their homes, many for the first time, during the war. For some like Pop, who would soon be shipped to the Philippines, Korea, and other locations on the war front, sadly, it would be their last holiday meal.

Today, as we all participate in the delights of these delicious dishes, I begin also to think of those throughout the country who do fall into the category of those defined officially as homeless. I know that other organizations in Anchorage, like the Salvation Army, provide a sumptuous meal for those who need it. I'm curious about the Skagway community and wonder if homelessness is a problem.

"I was wondering... are there actually homeless people here in Skagway?" I ask.

The woman sitting across from me replies, "I know of one in town in recent years who got food stamps, and she really did need them."

I'm surprised at such a low, almost infinitesimal, homeless rate since in Arkansas it's much higher. I remember my own family history when the church delivered a food basket the Christmas I was three. I think of Daddy as he was often fed and given shelter at the Union Gospel Rescue Missions. I think of one of my university colleagues who had just received his Ph.D. and taught at our school for one year. When contracts were re-issued in the spring, he did not receive one. Since I'm sure he found this fact embarrassing to admit to his folks back home in the northwest, he simply decided to drive his car to City Lake and live in it several months while he dealt with his shame and evaluated his options. None of our university faculty knew about it until several months after he had left for—hopefully-greener pastures. I know I felt doubly guilty. Garlan and I walk the same three-mile trek around that lake several times a week for exercise. I can see us now—obliviously chatting about other people and small things while, though out of sight, this man was without family or friends.

Today in America it's often easier to hide the homeless by getting them off the streets rather than addressing the root causes related to addictions, mental instability, and job loss. Certainly the mayor of New York just gave Hillary Clinton good political ammunition by having the police arrest one hundred homeless on the streets during this Thanksgiving holiday.

For me, the solution has always been found in the Word, and it's one that seems to be practiced by the community of Skagway. It's simply to take care of one's own. Jesus reminded the disciples through His teaching of this important command when He said, "for I was hungry and you gave Me food; I was thirsty and you gave Me drink; I was a stranger and you took Me in; I was naked and you clothed Me; I was sick and you visited Me; I was in prison and you came to Me" (Matt 25: 35–36).

As far as I can tell, this community has gotten it just about right.

Chapter Thirty-five
Arts and the Heart

On this Thanksgiving evening, we decide to go back into town for the classical concert with visiting musicians, Gilles Apap and Eric Ferrand-N'Kaoua. They are set to play several classical selections on the violin and the piano. The lights are soft in the church with an old lamp burning, which provide a soothing atmosphere for the Enescu, Debussy, and Ravel sonatas that we are about to hear. As is usual for us, we're the first ones to arrive. Soon, though, the church fills up with other lovers of good music.

The two musicians seem to be a bit of an oxymoron in that the pianist is dressed as one normally expects for a classical performance in a white suit, but the violinist looks as if he's still back in the late 60s playing in Greenwich Village. At one point, the violinist jokingly says the two of them have been together as performers for a year but that they hate each other. The music they have chosen complements their talents, however, and they play flawlessly. The violinist uses no music and often strolls through the aisles like one might expect to see and hear at a small café in France. At one point he sits on the steps up front with his legs crossed and his eyes closed as if lost in another era and time.

I often wonder about the motivation of these artists and the drive that compels these French musicians who make Atlin, Whitehorse, Skagway, and Haines a part of their concert tour. Admittedly, these towns need music of the heart to combat the effects of six hours of daylight in the winter, but the audiences must be small compared to cities like Anchorage, which they might have chosen instead. Are they like the players in Tom Stoppard's play *Rosencrantz and Guildenstern Are Dead?* When the two protagonists are out in the country, they run into the dramatic players who are on their way to entertain King Claudius, Gertrude, and Hamlet. The players are delighted and begin donning costumes and getting out props because they consider even two an audience. Or must they simply play for themselves whether there's an audience or not?

Today a lot of attention is being given to the state of the arts in America, whether it's controversy over the appropriateness of the latest art exhibition at the Metropolitan in New York, the advisability of keeping music as part of the public school curriculum (Meryl Streep's film *Music of the Heart*), or slashing creative writing programs because of budget constraints. As bad as the problem is here, it's far worse in other countries, like Russia for example. When several students, Kimberly, and I visited Kiev, Ukraine, in 1993, just two years after the dissolution of the Soviet bloc, there were starving artists (and art) everywhere. Classically trained musicians played on the streets with their hats at their feet, collecting whatever coins they could. The museums were dark with the lights being flipped off until visitors came through each room. Then the old babushkas would hop up like spry little bunnies, give us a bit of light, and become exuberant as they described the art exhibits to us from

"their" rooms. While we were there, we went to a Verdi opera, a
Chekhov play, *The Seagull*, a classical concert, and a ballet.
Taking ten of us to the opera cost a mere seventy-five cents of
American money. I wondered if the performers were even paid.

I tend to think, though, in spite of these concerns, that art
of the heart will never be restrained because of its hold over
us—it moves us in ways that simply cannot be explained or
rationalized.

After this concert, the next in the Skagway Arts Council
series features a folk musician, Marty Waldman, whose performance has been promoted for the whole family. Kids get in free. As
Garlan and I come into the church this night, we overhear a bit of
his personal story. He is telling Barb, the coordinator, "I'm Jewish,
and I always seem to be playing in Christian churches lately."
Maybe the rabbis care about such issues, but this man seems com-
pelled like the others to present his art wherever there's an audience. He soon sets up his guitar and banjo and begins teaching us
lyrics and encouraging all of us in the audience, even the old ones
like us, to sing along with him. Soon we're all doing hand motions
and singing "Puff, the Magic Dragon" and an old Russian song
(which we attempt to sing in Russian as well as in English), "May
there always be sunshine, May there always be blue skies, May
there always be Mama, May there always be me."

The Skagway children are at his feet, listening attentively to him, as if he is a pied piper, who has come to transfix
them with his music and whisk them away with him to the

next place. As I watch their fascination, I realize that the music is for them; they are the lovely children who will be the decision makers of tomorrow. Perhaps if we can truly keep them enthused by the arts, they too will realize that music of the heart can never be silenced.

Chapter Thirty-six
Innocence in Our Town

Today, as I sit in my pew (I've claimed one like the other locals) at church, I realize this is the last Sunday I'll be able to watch the expressions of Michael, who sits attentively each week during the Children's Moment with the pastor. I'm not sure of his age; I'm guessing eight or nine. He and his dad, Scott, lit the candles last week for the beginning of Advent. I know he's not perfect because I heard during one of the fellowships that he had recently put his sister's underwear in plastic baggies, filled them with water, and froze them. While Michael listens to the story this day with his whole heart, I've noticed he's also an interactive learner. He reminds me of myself and Billy Bruister back at First Baptist Church in Tutwiler in the early '50s. For example, the pastor recently used a lock and key as a visual aid with the children to teach them about the keys to the kingdom and that they were the most important part, of course. As he gave the children leading questions, he asked, "How many of you children would have had to walk to church this morning if your parents couldn't find the keys to the car?"

Several dutifully raised their hands. He continued, "What if you had taken a trip up to Whitehorse and gotten home only to discover you didn't have keys to your house, what would you do?"

At this point, like Billy and me, Michael pops up and says quickly, "Go around to the back door!" He got a good laugh from the church audience because of his naiveté, but I think also because everyone recognized the truth of what he had said.

Our town, Skagway, isn't Grovers Corners, New Hampshire at the turn of the century, but it's very similar in its innocence still. Unlike where we live in northwest Arkansas, where we've had a Jeep stolen and several CD players ripped out of automobiles, Skagwayans truly don't bother to lock their car doors or their houses. They know their stuff will be safe here.

I witnessed old-fashioned innocence again this past weekend with the Yuletide Festival, which is celebrated every year here as a community. I guess the celebration officially began as the town crier came through the Fire Hall (which was hosting an open house with cider and cookies), clanging his big bell and drawing all locals, young and old, to the tree-lighting ceremony at 5th and Broadway. Soon Mr. and Mrs. Santa Claus arrived, the community choir donned in their nineteenth-century costumes sang carols, the children sang "We Wish You a Merry Christmas," and the celebration began.

The evening was not exactly clear since a light snow was falling, but the temperature for Alaska in December was moderate, and the north wind wasn't blowing. The couple in front of me held their two-year-boy between them. As the carolers sang the father put his arm around his wife's waist, drew her nearer to him, and kissed her.

Everyone then went around to tour the three additional open houses downtown at the museum, mock saloon called The Mascot, and the White Pass & Yukon depot (which put on quite a spread with vegetables, fruits, cheeses, meats, and sweets). I'm tempted to also write, "A good time was had by all," which was our local paper's concluding line from the 1950s for all the local events. The next day's activities featured two bazaars, carnival, kids movie, and steak feed and ended with the Yuletide Ball which continued until midnight.

In today's society, we've heard the term "family values" so much recently that we've quickly tired of it, though not of the concept it represents. I pray that our town can always retain its innocence by continuing to value its young as well as its old, remembering as Emily so eloquently states in the conclusion to another famous Wilder play, *Our Town,* to continue "to look at each other, really really look at each other."

Chapter Thirty-seven
The Homecoming

We take our time and pack the car carefully on this day, December 13, since our ferry doesn't depart south to Bellingham, Washington, until 5:30. We arrive at the ferry terminal well before the one-hour-before-departure requirement. We have a few shots left on the camera and turn to capture a last glimpse of the snow-peaked mountains surrounding this tiny town of Skagway.

The name, "Home of the North Wind," has certainly been an accurate one since we have lain in our upstairs bedroom in the cabin many nights since our arrival, listening to its mournful howl outside our window. Its sound is like an Arctic wolf who has somehow become separated from her litter of pups.

Some days, after the snow began to fall for the season on October 16, we have girded our loins with down coats, fleece vests, parkas designed for below-zero temperatures, gloves, hats, and scarves for a walk downhill into town or a walk uphill to the lookout. At the lookout, we often pause longer than we should to enjoy the panoramic view of the town in the valley. It's the same lookout where Mam and Pop sat fifty-five years ago.

We see the mountains, of course, which encompass and envelope Skagway along with the icy water leading to points south. We see the air strip where the small Cessna, Beech, and Canadian airplanes fly in and out several times a day delivering their passengers to and from the capital of Juneau. We've watched these winged passenger birds fly beside our cabin window every day, marveling at their faithful tenacity to master and be victorious over the north wind.

Of course, as the odyssey ends and I begin the final journey toward home, I feel strangely ambivalent. Walking the same streets my grandparents walked, attending their church, and seeing the familiar spectacular postcard scenery in person is an experience I will remember for the remaining days God gives me. The odyssey has brought me incredibly closer to appreciating my heritage from my maternal line—Mam, Mama, Kimberly—and understanding our common struggles as women. It has also given me an admiration for those outside the bloodline—Pop and Nelson—and a realization of their importance as lifetime supporters of the women they loved. I've learned that family is not made up of blood relationships only. Family means love, and often sacrifice, for those within it—forming a bond that cannot be broken by even the strongest attacks against it. It truly is like the love of God to us as described in Romans 8:38–39: "…neither death, nor life, or angels, or principalities, nor powers, nor things present, nor things to come, / or height, or depth, or any other creature. shall be able to separate us …."

On the other hand, I'm excited that the journey—mentally, physically, and most importantly, spiritually—is almost over. It's been wrenching to dredge up the forgotten (or repressed) negative memories of childhood. But as I've confronted those, I've also gotten in touch with the child within me again. There really were the good memories as well—of Judy and our early years when she was more like a mother than a sister to me, of the great soul love between Mam and Pop that lasted over thirty earthly years, of God's faithfulness in healing Mama's heart, of my own God-ordained meeting, in answer to a mother's prayers, with a rock of a man as my life partner, and of our adult children, who are everything a mother could wish for.

As I stand on the deck of the ferry, I'm once more Odysseus or Ishmael returning home after the big adventure. Instead of Penelope or Telemachus, I go home instead—with my husband—to our Kimberly and Sheri in Seattle and Chris, Carrie, and Caitlyn in Little Rock. I believe I've won over the Cyclops, or the great white whale, and I'm ready to lay down my spear and make peace with those giants. I've also learned, along with Odysseus (and perhaps even Dorothy from Kansas), what is truly important in this life: "Where shall a man find sweetness to surpass / his own home and his parents? In far lands he shall not, though he find a house of gold."

Whether the time is away or close, I look forward to the greatest homecoming—with God, family, and friends who have gone on before me. With outstretched arms, He'll greet me, forgiving my questions and doubts, remembering only His grace and mercy. They'll also be waiting for me. We'll have so much to talk about.

Did I find my search for the Aurora, one might ask? Each one must experience it to understand its beckoning. Suffice it to say, "The north wind has ceased; the tempest has stopped." I invite all who need peace and healing to try a spiritual journey as well.